MW00653094

The Virginia Drug Crime
Defense Manual

1st Edition

Luke J. Nichols, Esq.
Garrett D. Green, Esq.

For questions and comments, contact:

Luke J. Nichols or Garrett D. Green at
The law firm of Nichols & Green pllc
(703) 383-9222 (phone)
(703) 383-9220 (fax)
lnichols@nicholsgreen.com
ggreen@nicholsgreen.com
www.nicholsgreen.com

ISBN: 978-0-9828928-5-5

Spectrum Publishing
Fairfax, Va

Table of Contents

Introduction

Possession of a controlled substance is the most common felony charge in Virginia. Each day hundreds of people are arrested for possession of a controlled substance in Virginia.

From kingpin drug dealers to high school students, the Commonwealth of Virginia comes down hard on anyone charged with a drug crime.

Most drug charges come with mandatory license suspensions and many result in jail time and probation. The immigration consequences of any drug charge can be devastating. And a drug conviction in Virginia will remain on a defendant's criminal record forever.

Despite the severe consequences of a drug arrest, a large number of defendants come to court uninformed and unprepared. They do not know their rights, they do not understand the legal process, they do not have confidence in their lawyer, and they do not know how to use their attorney effectively.

The purpose of this book is to inform and empower anyone charged with violating Virginia's drug laws. This book will discuss each of the drug laws, their consequences, the judicial process, common defenses, the various court programs, the pros and cons of cooperating with detectives, and how to choose and work with a qualified criminal defense attorney.

The best criminal defense attorneys understand the complex and changing constitutional and forensic issues involved in most drug cases. The best criminal defense attorneys have ample trial experience. And the best criminal defense attorneys take the time to get to know their client and to communicate the information contained in this book.

If you or someone you love has been arrested for a drug crime I hope that you will take the time to read this book. Educated defendants not only hire better attorneys, they get more out of the attorneys they hire.

Chapter 1
Which Laws and Which Courts Apply?

The Virginia legal system can be complicated. A single drug transaction can break multiple laws in multiple jurisdictions. Knowing which laws apply, which courts have jurisdiction, and how the Virginia court system is organized is a first step in understanding the legal process.

Which Laws Apply?
To know the law, you must first know who is enforcing the laws. There are several levels of government: city/town, county, state and federal. Each level of government may have its own laws, and each may have its own police force.

The FBI, DEA, and federal police forces enforce federal laws. State troopers enforce state law. The county police and sheriff's department enforce state and county laws. The municipal police enforce municipal ordinances but they can also charge people under state laws. Other law enforcement officers, such as university police, usually only enforce state laws.

In the Commonwealth of Virginia there are 95 counties and 39 independent cities (such as Alexandria, Fairfax City, and Falls Church). Inside those counties are towns which may have their own semi-independent judicial system (such as Vienna, Haymarket, and Herndon).

Each county, independent city or town has the ability to create laws in addition to those created by the level of government above them. Consequently, if you are arrested for possession of marijuana, you can be charged with violating the state law, the county code, or perhaps even a town or city ordinance.

Federal laws can apply anytime drug activity crosses state lines. Federal laws or federal courts may also be involved if the crime occurred on federal property.

Crimes committed in national parks fall under the jurisdiction of the National Park Service. Crimes in national parks are tried in federal courts and punished under federal law (i.e. the Code of Federal Regulations).

However, crimes committed by civilians on military bases in Virginia or on federal facilities such as the Pentagon are tried under the laws of the Commonwealth of Virginia, even though the trials take place in federal courts.

State, county, and city drug laws are usually the same but sometimes there can be major differences. It is always very important to present your summons or arrest warrant to your attorney so he or she can know exactly which law you are being charged with violating and in which jurisdiction you are required to appear.

Despite the many differences in state, county, city, and federal laws, the vast majority of defendants are charged under the state laws of Virginia or under local laws that are substantially similar to the state laws.

Consequently, for the sake of space, this book will only cover Virginia's state laws.

Which Court Has Jurisdiction?
Before you can be convicted, the court you are in has to have jurisdiction over your case. To have jurisdiction, the defendant must have broken the laws of that particular jurisdiction. A Virginia court cannot enforce federal laws or the law of another state.

Additionally, some portion of the crime must have occurred within the borders of the court's jurisdiction. You cannot be tried in Fairfax County for possession of marijuana that occurred *only* in Arlington County. But if a person has weed in their pocket and drives from Arlington to Fairfax County, then they could be tried for possession in either Fairfax or Arlington County.

When a criminal act crosses state, county, or city lines it can become difficult to predict which court has the jurisdiction. Sometimes multiple courts may attempt to charge the same defendant for the same crime. This may be a violation of the defendant's constitutional rights against double jeopardy.

The US and Virginia Constitution
The rights of citizens inside the Commonwealth of Virginia come from the laws of Virginia, the Constitution of Virginia, and the US Constitution's Bill of Rights (also known as the amendments).

Many of the laws governing searches, seizures, arrests, interrogations, attorneys, and trials are recorded in the first 14 amendments to the US Constitution.

Virginia has a very similar constitution and bill of rights that apply only in Virginia, while the US Constitution applies in all states.

The Virginia Court System
In Virginia, there are four levels of courts: General District Court, Circuit Court, the Court of Appeals, and the Virginia Supreme Court.

General District Court (GDC) is where misdemeanor trials occur and were felony arraignments and felony preliminary hearings are held. There are no juries in GDC. Juvenile and Domestic Relations Court (JDR) is a specialized General District Court for defendants who are juveniles and cases involving crimes against family members or minors.

Circuit Court is where felonies are tried. Misdemeanor cases can be appealed from GDC to Circuit Court. Either the Commonwealth or the defendant can demand a jury trial in Circuit Court.

The Court of Appeals does not hold trials; it only hears appeals from Circuit Court. And the Virginia Supreme Court mostly hears appeals from the Court of Appeals.

When you are looking for an attorney make sure your attorney clearly states which courts they will represent you in. Many attorneys charge a lot more money to go from one court to the next even though your case may not be completed.

Chapter 2
Virginia's Judicial Process

Felony vs. Misdemeanor
The judicial process is very different depending on whether you have been charged with a felony or a misdemeanor. In addition, the consequences of conviction are different for felonies versus misdemeanors.

Both are crimes and both remain on your criminal record forever. Felons can go to prison for more than one year and can be banned from voting. They cannot own guns and cannot serve on a jury. Felonies carry much more of social stigma and most job applications ask whether you have ever been convicted of a felony.

Felonies are much more likely to affect your immigration status, security clearance, and military service.

In Virginia, a single misdemeanor can never result in more than 12 months in jail, and misdemeanors usually do not affect your civil rights (voting, gun ownership, etc.). Misdemeanors can affect employment, immigration, and security clearances as well, but often to a lesser extent.

Judicial Process for Misdemeanors
If you are charged with a misdemeanor, your case begins with an arrest. An arrest can involve receiving a Virginia Uniform Summons without being put in handcuffs. Or it may involve a ride to the police station.

Whether you are taken to jail or released with a summons, misdemeanors begin in General District Court (GDC) for adults and in Juvenile and Domestic Relations Court (JDR) for minors and adult cases involving victims who are family members or minors.

When a crime involves the possibility of jail time, a judge must inform the defendant of their constitutional right to an attorney. For more serious criminal charges the judge does this at a special hearing called an arraignment. If the defendant is locked up in jail, the arraignment may be done by a videoconference from jail.

Some jurisdictions skip the arraignment for some minor misdemeanor charges. And some jurisdictions will skip the arraignment if the defendant hires an attorney before the arraignment hearing.

After the arraignment, the next hearing for misdemeanors is usually the trial. If the defendant is not happy with the outcome of the trial, he or she can appeal the judge's decision to the Circuit Court for any reason within 10 days of the trial in GDC or JDR.

Pending appeal, the defendant will be innocent again, and will owe the court no fines, no court cost, will get their license back, and will usually be released from jail. The Circuit Court will have a completely new trial and the Circuit Court judge will not even know what happened in the first trial.

The prosecution or the defendant can choose to have a jury trial in Circuit Court, though defendants should consult with an attorney before deciding whether to have a jury. Jury trials are much more complicated, more expensive, and juries in Virginia get to decide the punishment in criminal cases. Virginia Juries are notorious for imposing very severe punishments for some crimes.

If the defendant is not happy with the outcome in Circuit Court, he can try to appeal to the Virginia Court of Appeals and then to the Virginia Supreme Court. Both of these courts can choose whether or not they want to hear the appeal and neither holds trials.

To win an appeal at the Virginia Court of Appeals or the Virginia Supreme Court, the Circuit Court judge must have made a significant mistake while acting as judge. These appeals are not automatically granted.

Most misdemeanors take two to four months to get through General District Court or Juvenile and Domestic Relations Court. However, in extreme cases or in cases that require laboratory testing of drugs, getting through GDC or JDR court can take four to eight months. Very few cases take longer. An appeal to Circuit Court typically takes another one to three months.

On rare occasions the prosecution can skip GDC or JDR court and go straight to Circuit Court. This is called a "direct indictment." This often happens when a defendant has both misdemeanor and felony charges at the same time. The prosecution may direct indict the misdemeanors so that all the charges (misdemeanor and felony) can be tried at the same time in Circuit Court.

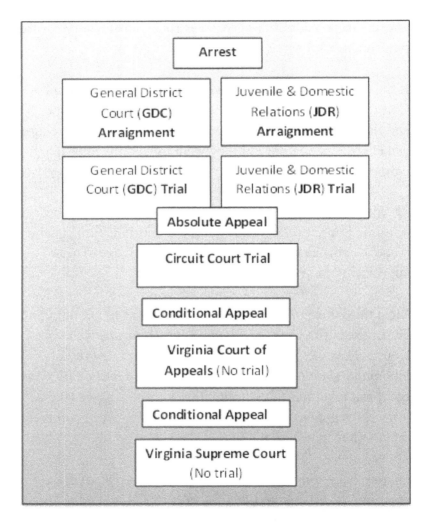

Judicial Process for Misdemeanors

Judicial Process for Felonies

If you are charged with a felony, your case will take a lot more time and more court appearances. The exact process and requirements for the felony judicial process varies considerably from jurisdiction to jurisdiction, but this section outlines some of the steps that are common to most jurisdictions in Virginia.

Like a misdemeanor case, felonies begin with arrests, followed by an arraignment in General District Court or Juvenile and Domestic Relations Court. At the arraignment, the judge will advise the Defendant of their constitutional right to an attorney.

After the arraignment, the next felony hearing is the preliminary hearing in GDC or JDR. Preliminary hearings look and sound like a normal trial, but they are not.

At a preliminary hearing, the judge is not deciding whether a Defendant is guilty or innocent. At a preliminary hearing, the judge is only trying to determine whether the government has the minimum evidence necessary (sufficient "probable cause") to justify advancing the case to circuit court.

During the preliminary hearing the judge is required to interpret the evidence in a light most favorable to the prosecution whenever possible. After hearing the prosecution's evidence, the judge asks himself whether the prosecution's evidence is sufficient enough that a reasonable jury could possibly find the defendant guilty.

If the judge believes the evidence is sufficient, then the judge sends the case to the Circuit Court and a grand jury. If the judge does not believe the evidence is sufficient, the case is dismissed.

However, if the case is dismissed at the preliminary hearing stage, the prosecution can elect to directly indict the defendant and take the case straight to Circuit Court. This type of direct indictment is rare.

The preliminary hearing is also the defense attorney's first opportunity to negotiate with the prosecution and the first opportunity to take or reject a deal from the prosecution. Many felony cases are resolved at the preliminary hearing after the defendant accepts a deal.

If the defendant rejects the deal and loses the preliminary hearing, the case is sent to Circuit court for another hearing called a "term date."

A "term date" is a very short simple hearing that is similar to an arraignment. You show up to court, the judge checks whether you have complied with the conditions of your bond, and the judge sets a date for your trial. Failure to appear for the term date can result in a bench warrant, additional criminal charges, and revocation of your bond.

At the term date the defendant and the prosecution must decide whether to have the trial in front of a jury or just a judge (called a bench trial). Either the prosecution or the defendant can ask for a jury trial. Always talk to your attorney about the pros and cons of having a jury. Juries cost more money, take more time, and in Virginia juries frequently impose harsher punishments than judges.

If the defendant wins the trial, they go free. If the defendant is convicted then the judge will set a sentencing date to determine the appropriate punishment.

If the defendant accepts a plea to a felony and waives the preliminary hearing, then there is usually no term day and instead the defendant is assigned a plea date where the judge will ask the defendant a series of questions to determine whether or not they are pleading guilty to the charge freely, voluntarily, and intelligently.

If the judge accepts the guilty plea and everything goes smoothly, then the judge will set a sentencing date.

Prior to the sentencing date, the defendant will be asked to meet with a probation officer. The probation officer will collect the defendant's adult and juvenile criminal records, interview the defendant, and then create a pre-sentencing report that will be delivered to the prosecution, the defense, and the judge.

The pre-sentencing report will contain a background report about the defendant and a multi-page mathematical formula called the Virginia Sentencing Guidelines. The sentencing guidelines will give the judge a range of recommended punishments that the judge can choose to follow or ignore.

The interview with the probation officer, the sentencing guidelines, and the sentencing report are very important.

Always consult with your attorney before your interview to make sure you are properly prepared. The interview with the probation officer can be more important than the sentencing date itself.

Drug or alcohol testing and screening may occur at your pre-sentencing interview. Failing one of these drug or alcohol tests may result in additional jail time, so always refrain from drug or alcohol use while on bond or pretrial release. If you do not believe you can refrain from using drugs or alcohol 100 percent for the months you are pending trial or while on probation, discuss it with your attorney.

Because of how complicated these reports can be, it is common for pre-sentencing reports and sentencing guidelines to contain errors that can result in additional jail time. Make sure you review your pre-sentencing report and sentencing guidelines with your attorney with plenty of time prior to the sentencing hearing.

At the sentencing hearing, the judge will review the pre-sentencing report and listen to arguments from the defense and the prosecution before issuing the sentence. The judge can follow the Sentencing Guideline recommendations or the judge can ignore then.

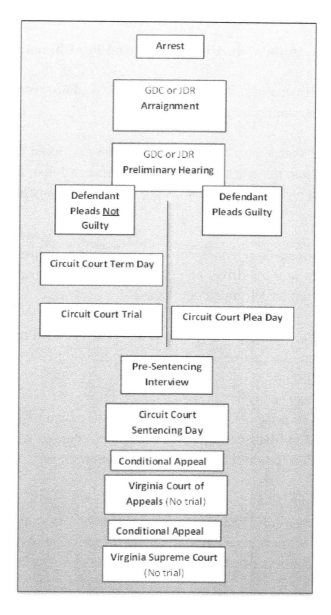

Judicial Process for Felonies

Chapter 3
Virginia's Marijuana Laws and Punishment

Yes, marijuana is still illegal in Virginia. And no, you can't get a prescription here either.

Virginia's marijuana laws are full of surprises. Even the smallest and insignificant bit of marijuana residue or ash is illegal. If a police officer can test it, you can get arrested for it.

All marijuana convictions come with a six-month loss of license even if the driver enters the first offender diversion program under Virginia code 18.2-251.

Possessing synthetic marijuana is more serious than real marijuana. And growing marijuana can result in five to 30 years in prison.

Another surprise is that there is no minimum quantity threshold for distribution. A person can be charged with distribution for sharing the scrapings from their pipe.

Possession of Marijuana
Va Code § 18.2-250.1 makes it a crime to possess any quantity of marijuana without a valid prescription. And a doctor cannot prescribe marijuana in Virginia.

It is a misdemeanor to possess marijuana. A first offense has a maximum penalty of 30 days in jail, a $500 fine, and a six-month loss of driving privileges. A second offense has a maximum penalty of 12 months in jail, $2,500 in fines, and a six-month loss of license.

First-time marijuana possession is a criminal offense and a conviction will go on a one's criminal record forever. There is no way to expunge a criminal conviction in Virginia, even if the charge is later dismissed as part of a first offender program.

Marijuana resin, tar, residue, ash and most parts of the plant are treated as marijuana according to Va. Code § 54.1-3401. Mature marijuana stalks are not considered to be marijuana under Virginia law, but only if the stalks are not combined with any other illegal part of the marijuana plant.

Because of this law, the police can charge a person with possession if they have even the tiniest amount of residue or ash on a pipe, bong, or grinder. If you have a dirty pipe, bong, grinder, or a similar item, then you can be charged with possession of marijuana.

Possession of marijuana requires the government to prove two things: 1) that the substance was marijuana and 2) that the defendant possessed it.

Proving that a substance is marijuana requires field or laboratory testing. Marijuana testing presents complicated evidentiary and legal issues.

Proving possession requires proving 1) that the defendant knew that the marijuana was in their control and 2) that the defendant knew the item was marijuana.

Possession with the Intent to Distribute (PWID) Marijuana
Va Code § 18.2-248.1 outlaws possession with intent to
distribute marijuana, or "PWID-marijuana" for short
(pronounced "pee-wid").

There are several ways the police attempt to prove
possession with intent to distribute: undercover drug buys,
confessions, text messages from the defendant's phone, the
quantity of drugs (more than the amount typical for personal
use), possession of scales, individually packaged drugs and
possession of lots of cash.

The punishments for PWID-marijuana increase as the
quantity of marijuana in the defendant's possession
increases. However, there is no minimum quantity for
PWID-marijuana. One officer I know made a PWID arrest
after he witnessed one man pass a joint to another man while
they were smoking weed on a stoop.

PWID up to .5 ounces of marijuana is a misdemeanor with a
maximum of 12 months in jail and a mandatory six-month
license suspension.

PWID more than .5 ounces and less than five pounds of
marijuana is a felony with a maximum of 10 years in jail
and a mandatory six-month license suspension.

PWID more than five pounds of marijuana (but less than
100 kg) is a felony with a maximum of 30 years in jail and a
minimum of five years in prison.

PWID of 100 kilograms or more of marijuana is a felony punishable by 20 years to life in prison. If you have been arrested for possession with intent to distribute over 100 kilograms of marijuana, you probably do not need this book to know you are in trouble.

PWID Near a School
Va Code § 18.2-255.2 bans possessing drugs with the intent to distribute (PWID) near schools, day care centers, school bus stops, and many other public locations. This law applies even if the defendant was not intending to distribute the drugs on school property.

For example, if a suspect is arrested for PWID while driving through a school zone, they may be guilty of PWID near a school.

There is a long list of locations where this statute applies: any public property within 1,000 feet of a school, including colleges and junior colleges, day care centers, recreation centers, public libraries, community centers; within 1,000 feet of a school bus stop if children are there; any public property within 1,000 feet of a state hospital or health facility.

Growing Marijuana
Growing, producing, preparing, propagating, compounding, converting, or processing marijuana that is not just for personal use is a felony with a maximum fine of $1,000,000 and a maximum of 30 years in prison with a five-year minmum .There are no minimum quantity requirements. A

person can be guilty of this serious felony for growing a single plant and giving a home-grown joint to a friend.

Possession of Drug Paraphernalia
The only items that count as drug paraphernalia under Va. Code 54.1-3466 are syringes and items used for injecting drugs. Scales, grinders, bongs, etc. are not paraphernalia under this statute.

However, this statute is often used by defense attorneys as a substitute for many other drug crimes. This charge is a popular plea deal because it won't result in a license suspension. People who need to drive may prefer a conviction for paraphernalia rather than a conviction of any of the other drug crimes.

A prosecutor and defense attorney can agree to amend a drug charge to possession of paraphernalia even if the defendant did not possess any syringes, but only if both the defense attorney and the prosecution agree.

Possession of Synthetic Marijuana (Spice or K2)
Synthetic marijuana (also called *K2* or *Spice*), is an industrial insulator that causes a high when smoked. For several years it was not illegal and was openly packaged and sold in stores as synthetic "legal" marijuana.

In 2011 the Virginia legislature outlawed a long list of synthetic compounds used in knockoff marijuana. By the time this law was passed, fake weed was being sold openly and legally online and in gas stations in Virginia.

Many people are still ignorant of this law and some seller still sell synthetic marijuana openly without knowing (or caring) that it has been outlawed.

As the time this book is being written there are currently no field test kits for synthetic marijuana. The police and synthetic marijuana users have difficultly knowing which types of synthetic marijuana contain the now illegal substances. Laboratory testing is currently the only way of identifying illegal synthetic marijuana.

The penalties for synthetic marijuana are much more severe than the penalties for possession of real marijuana. First time possession of synthetic marijuana is a Class 1 misdemeanor with penalties of up to 12 months in jail. Possession with intent to distribute (PWID) synthetic marijuana is a felony that comes with up to five years in prison.

Marijuana Punishment Chart

Code Section	Description	Type of Crime	Max Jail	Minimum Jail.	Mandatory Min.	Max Fine	License suspension
18.2-250.1	Possession (1st offense)	Misdemeanor	30 days	NA		$500	6 months
18.2-250.1	Possession (2nd offense)	Misdemeanor	12 mths	NA		$2,500	6 months
18.2-248.1(a)(1)	PWID 0.5 oz or less	Misdemeanor	12 mths	NA		$2,500	6 months
18.2-248.1(a)(2)	PWID 0.6 oz to 5 lbs	Felony	10 years	NA		$2,500	6 months
18.2-248.1(a)(3)	PWID 5.1 lbs or more	Felony	30 years	5 years		$2,500	6 months
18.2-248.1(a)	PWID (not for profit)	Misdemeanor	12 mths	NA		$2,500	6 months
18.2-248.1(b)	PWID to inmate (not for profit)	Felony	10 years	2 years		$100,000	6 months
18.2-248.1(c)	Growing/Manufacture (non personal use)	Felony	30 years	5 years		$10,000	6 months
18.2-248.1(d)	3rd felony 18.2-248.1 offense	Felony	Life	5 years		$500,000	6 months
18.2-248(H)(4)	PWID 100 kilos or more	Felony	Life	20 years*		$1,000,000	6 months
18.2-248(H1)(4)	Criminal Enterprise with 100-250 Kilos	Felony	Life	20 years		$1,000,000	6 months
18.2-248(H2)(4)	Criminal Enterprise with 250 kilos or more	Felony	Life	Life*		$1,000,000	6 months
18.2-248.01	PWID & Transportation into Virginia	Felony	40 years	5 years		$1,000,000	6 months
18.2-248.01	PWID & Transportation into Virginia (2nd)	Felony	40 years	10 years		$1,000,000	6 months
18.2-255	Distribution to a Minor	Felony	50 years	10 year	5yrs/2yrs*	$100,000	6 months
18.2-255.2	PWID on school property	Felony	5 years	1 year		$100,000	6 months
18.2-255.2	PWID on school property (2nd)	Felony	5 years	1 year	1year	$100,000	6 months
18.2-255.2	PWID on school property (not for profit)	Misdemeanor	12 mths	NA		$2,500	6 months
54.1-3466	Possession of drug paraphernalia	Misdemeanor	12 mths	0	0	$2,500	NA
18.2-248.1:1	Possession Synthetic Marijuan (Spice or K-2)	Misdemeanor	12 mths	0	0	$2,500	6 months
18.2-248.1:1	PWID Synthetic Marijuan (Spice or K-2)	Felony	5 yrs	0 yrs	0	$2,500	6 months
18.2-248.1:1	Manufacturing Synthetic Marijuan (Spice or K-2)	Felony	30 yrs	5 yrs	0 yrs	$10,000	6 months

Chapter 4
Virginia's Non-Marijuana Drug Laws and Punishments

Possession of a Controlled Substance (Non-Marijuana)
Va. Code § 18.2-250 makes it illegal to possess any controlled substance without a valid prescription.

- Possession of a Schedule I or II drug is a Class 5 felony with up to 10 years in prison and a $2,500 fine.
- Possessing a Schedule III drug is a Class 1 misdemeanor with up to 12 months in jail and a $2,500 fine.
- Possession of a Schedule IV drug is a Class 2 misdemeanor with up to six months in jail and a $1000 fine.
- Possession of a Schedule V drug is a Class 3 misdemeanor with a maximum fine of $500.
- Possession of a Schedule VI drug is a Class 4 misdemeanor with a maximum fine of $250.

The vast majority of street drugs are Schedule I/II drugs. Prescription drugs that are used recreationally are Schedule II, III, IV and V. Schedule VI drugs include all remaining prescription drugs that are not in one of the other schedules. Schedule VI drugs are generally prescription drugs that have no recreational value.

Possession with Intent to Distribute a Controlled Substance
Va. Code § 18.2-248 creates a special felony for possession with the intent to distribute a controlled substance.

There are several ways the police attempt to prove possession with intent to distribute (PWID): undercover drug buys, confessions, text messages from the defendant's phone, the quantity of drugs (more than the amount typical for personal use), possession of scales, individually packaged drugs, and possession of lots of cash.

The punishments for PWID non-marijuana increase as the quantity of drug in the defendant's possession increases. However, there is no minimum quantity for PWID-non-marijuana. An officer can charge someone if they share one hit on a crack pipe or pass around a needle.

PWID Schedule I,II, III, and IV drugs is a felony. PWID Schedule I/II drugs comes with up to 40 years in prison for the first offense and life in prison for the second offense with a mandatory minimum of three years. For the third offense, PWID Schedule I/II comes with a maximum of life in prison and a minimum of 10 years. Possession with intent to distribute is always a very serious crime.

PWID Near a School
Va Code § 18.2-255.2 bans PWID near schools, day care centers, school bus stops, and many other public locations. This law applies even if the defendant was not intending to distribute the drugs on school property.

For instance: if a defendant drives through a school zone while dropping some pills off at his friend's house, he has violated this statute.

There is a long list of locations where this statute applies: any public property within 1,000 feet of any school, including colleges and junior colleges, school bus stops (if children are present), day care centers, recreation centers, public libraries, community centers, and any public property within 1,000 feet of a state hospital or health facility.

To charge an individual with PWID, the police must prove the intent to distribute the drugs. The most common ways the police prove distribution is through text messages, voice mail messages, police stings, undercover informants, and statements by the defendant.

Possessing scales, several small individually wrapped quantities of drugs, large amounts of cash in small bills, and hanging out in a high drug-crime area can also be used as evidence to suggest distribution.

However, it is important to remember that the government must prove that the defendant intended to distribute the specific drugs he possessed at the time.

For example, if the police catch a suspect with .6 ounces of cocaine and a text message offering to sell 10 ecstasy pills, that may not be enough to prove PWID .6 ounces of cocaine.

Also, if a suspect is caught with .2 ounces of cocaine and a text message from a week ago offering to sell some cocaine, that text message may be too old to prove that the suspect possessed the .2 ounces with the intent to distribute.

Definition of Schedule I, II, III, IV, and V Drugs
The federal government defines which drugs fall under which schedule. Virginia law has also adopted these federal laws. The following is a list of just some of the common drugs, listed by schedule. This list does not include all drugs.

Virginia Drug Schedules		
Schedule I	**Schedule II**	**Schedule III**
Heroin	Opium	Anabolic Steroids (Oxandrin)
LSD	Crystal Meth	Vicodin
peyote	Cocaine	Lorcet
Ecstacy	Crack	Tylenol or Asprin with codeine
MDMA	Methadone	Ketamine (*Special K*)
GHB	morphine	
Meth	Oxycodone (OxyContin)	
Rohypnol (*Roofy*)*	Demerol	
	Adderall	
	Ritalin	
	PCP	
Schedule IV	**Schedule V**	**Schedule VI**
diazepam (Valium)	Robitussin AC	Any prescription drugs not
Rohypnol (*Roofy*)*	Phenergan with Codeine	included under the other
Xanax		schedules.
Talwin		
Equanil		
clonazepam (Klonopin)		

*Rohypnol is a Schedule IV drug but is punished as if it was a Schedule I drug

26

Non-Marijuana Drug Punishment Chart

Code Section	Description	Type of Crime	Max Jail	Minimum Jail.	Mandatory Min.	Max Fine	License suspension
18.2-250	Possession Schedule I/II	Felony	10 yr	0 yr	0 yr	$2,500	6 months
18.2-250	Possession Schedule III	Misdemeanor	12 mth	0 dy	0 dy	$2,500	6 months
18.2-250	Possession Schedule IV	Misdemeanor	6 mth	0 dy	0 dy	$1,000	6 months
18.2-250	Possession Schedule V	Misdemeanor	NA	NA	NA	$500	6 months
18.2-250	Possession Schedule VI	Misdemeanor	NA	NA	NA	$250	6 months
18.2-248	PWID Schedule I/II	Felony	40 yr	5 yr	0	$500,000	6 months
18.2-248	PWID Schedule I/II (2nd offense)	Felony	Life	5 yr	3 yr	$500,000	6 months
18.2-248	PWID Schedule I/II (3rd offense)	Felony	Life	10 yr	10 yr	$500,000	6 months
18.2-248	PWID 100 grs or more Heroine mixture	Felony	Life	5 yr	5 yr*	$1,000,000	6 months
18.2-248	PWID 500 grs or more Cocaine mixture	Felony	Life	5 yr	5 yr*	$1,000,000	6 months
18.2-248	PWID 20 grs or more of Meth mixture	Felony	Life	5 yr	5 yr*	$1,000,000	6 months
18.2-248	PWID 10 grs or more of Meth	Felony	Life	5 yr	5 yr*	$1,000,000	6 months
18.2-248	PWID 250 grs or more of Cocaine based mixture	Felony	Life	5 yr	5 yr*	$1,000,000	6 months
18.2-248 (C1)	Manufacturing 0-200 grs Meth mixture	Felony	40 yrs	10 yr	0	$500,000	6 months
18.2-248 (C1)	Manufacturing 0-200 grs Meth mixture (2nd offense)	Felony	Life	10 yr	0 yr	$500,000	6 months
18.2-248 (C1)	Manufacturing 0-200 grs Meth mixture (3rd offense)	Felony	Life	10 yr	3 yr	$500,000	6 months

27

Non-Marijuana Drug Punishment Chart

Code Section	Description	Type of Crime	Max Jail	Minimum Jail.	Mandatory Min.	Max Fine	License suspension
18.2-248 (D)	PWID Schedule I/II as an accomodation only	Felony	10 yr	0 yr	0 yr	$2,500	6 months
18.2-248 (E1)	PWID Schedule III (Except Anabolic Steroids)	Felony	10 yr	0 yr	0 yr	$2,500	6 months
18.2-248 (E2)	PWID Schedule IV	Felony	5 yr	0 yr	0 yr	$2,500	6 months
18.2-248 (E3)	PWID Schedule III/IV as an Accomodation only	Misdemeanor	12 mth	0 yr	0 yr	$2,500	6 months
18.2-248 (F)	PWID Schedule V/VI	Misdemeanor	12 mth	0 yr	0 yr	$2,500	6 months
18.2-248 (G)	PWID Immitation Schedule I,II,III,IV	Felony	5 yr	0 yr	0 yr	$2,500	6 months
18.2-248 (H)	PWID 1 K or more Heroine mixture	Felony	Life	20 yr	20 yr*	$1,000,000	6 months
18.2-248 (H)	PWID 5 K or more Cocaine mixture	Felony	Life	20 yr	20 yr*	$1,000,000	6 months
18.2-248 (H)	PWID 200 grs or more of Meth mixture	Felony	Life	20 yr	20 yr*	$1,000,000	6 months
18.2-248 (H)	PWID 100 grs or more of Meth	Felony	Life	20 yr	20 yr*	$1,000,000	6 months
18.2-248 (H)	PWID 2.5 K or more of Cocaine based mixture	Felony	Life	20 yr	20 yr*	$1,000,000	6 months
18.2-255.2	PWID on school property	Felony	5 years	1 year	0 yr	$100,000	6 months
18.2-255.2	PWID on school property (2nd)	Felony	5 years	1 year	1 year	$100,000	6 months
18.2-255.2	PWID on school property (not for profit)	Misdemeanor	12 mth	0 dy	0 dy	$2,500	6 months
18.2-248.03	PWID Meth mixture, 28 grs or more	Felony	40 yrs	5 yr	0	$500,000	6 months
18.2-248.03	PWID Meth mixture, 227 grs or more	Felony	Life	5 yr	5 yr	$1,000,000	6 months
54.1-3466	Possession of drug paraphenelia	Misdemeanor	12 mths	0	0	$2,500	NA

Chapter 5
Miscellaneous Drug Laws and Punishments

Obtaining Drugs by Fraud, Prescription Fraud, and Making a Fake Prescription

Va. Code 18.2-258.1 outlaws most conceivable ways that a person can attempt to get drugs by fraud, forgery, or deceit. Some of the common ways people commit this crime include:

- Making, using, or attempting to use fake prescriptions
- Using a fake name or ID to get or fill a prescription
- Using fake prescription labels (for example, on pill bottles)
- Stealing prescription drugs or prescriptions from an employer
- Lying to a physician about one's health in order to get a prescription

However, this law does not outlaw simply possessing a fake prescription, even if you know it's fake.

This law also does not ban attempting to fill another person's prescription as long as a fake ID or false information was not used.

Obtaining drugs by fraud is a felony in Virginia and comes with up to five years in prison and a six-month loss of license.

Possession of Drug Paraphernalia

Possession of drug paraphernalia under Va. Code 54.1-3466 is a misdemeanor criminal charge in Virginia. But it is one of the few drug charges that does not come with a 6-month loss of driving privileges.

The only items that count as drug paraphernalia under Va. Code 54.1-3466 are syringes and items used for injecting drugs. Scales, grinders, bongs, etc. are not paraphernalia under this statute.

However, this statute is often used by defense attorneys as substitute for many other drug crimes. This charge is a popular plea deal because it won't result in a license suspension. People who need to drive may prefer a conviction for paraphernalia rather than a conviction for any other drug crimes.

Possession of Synthetic Marijuana (Spice or K2)

Synthetic marijuana (also called *K2* or *Spice*), is an industrial insulator that causes a high when smoked. For several years it was not illegal and was openly packaged and sold in stores as synthetic "legal" marijuana.

In 2011, the Virginia legislature outlawed a long list of synthetic compounds used in synthetic marijuana. Prior to the passage of this law, fake weed was sold openly and legally online and in gas stations in Virginia.

Many people are still ignorant of this law and some still sell synthetic marijuana openly without knowing (or caring) that it has been outlawed.

At this writing, there are currently no field test kits for synthetic marijuana. It is difficult for the police and synthetic marijuana users to know whether a particular form of synthetic marijuana contains one of the now illegal substances. Currently, laboratory testing is the only way to know whether a particular form of synthetic marijuana is illegal. These ambiguities have opened the door to several possible defenses.

The penalties for synthetic marijuana are much more severe than the penalties for possession of real marijuana. First-time possession of synthetic marijuana is a Class 1 misdemeanor with penalties of up to 12 months in jail. PWID synthetic marijuana is a felony that comes with up to five years in prison.

Transporting Drugs into Virginia
Transporting more than one ounce of a Schedule I/II drug into Virginia for distribution is a serious crime in Virginia. This felony comes with a maximum penalty of 40 years in prison and a minimum of three. The maximum fine for violating Va. Code 18.2-248.01 is $1,000,000.

Transporting drugs across state lines can also result in federal drug charges and even more serious federal punishments.

Aiding in Illegally Obtaining Prescription Drugs

To be guilty of aiding others in illegally obtaining prescription drugs, you must get paid for your assistance. The payment can be money, favors, or goods, but the government must prove you did it for payment.

This law also requires that you know that the drugs were being obtained illegally. A common example of this is when a pharmacist or doctor sells drugs to people without a prescription or writes a bogus prescription for money.

Maintaining a Fortified Drug House
Violation of this law is much more common than people realize. Anytime an individual substantially alters a building used for making or selling drugs in order to prevent the police from entering, a crime is committed. Installing a large, heavy door that the police can't kick down may be an example. However, leaning stuff against the door or even nailing boards across the door does not qualify as a violation of this law.

Maintaining a fortified drug house is a felony with a maximum of 10 years in prison. This punishment is in addition to whatever drug charges may be brought.

Miscellaneous Drug Punishment Chart

Code Section	Description	Type of Crime	Max Jail	Minimum Jail.	Mandatory Min.	Max Fine	License suspension
18.2-248.02	Child present while manufacturing of meth	Felony	40 yrs	10 yr	0	$2,500	6 months
18.2-248.01	Transporting to Va 1 oz or more Schedule I/II	Felony	40 yr	5 yr	3 yr	$1,000,000	6 months
18.2-248.5	PWID Anabolic Steroids	Felony	10 yr	6 mth	6 mth	$20,000	6 months
18.2-248.5 (B)	Distribution Caffine & Ephedrinw Sulfate to a minor	Misdemeanor	12 mths	0	0	$2,500	6 months
18.251.3	PWID GBL (Gamma-butyrolactone)	Felony	20 yrs	5 yrs	0	$2,500	6 months
18.2-251.4	Cheating a Drug Test	Misdemeanor	12 mths	0	0	$100,000	6 months
18.2-258.02	Maintaning a Fortified Drug House	Felony	10 yrs	0 yrs	0 yrs	$2,500	6 months
18.2-258.1	Obtaining Drugs by forgery, fraud, or deceit	Felony	5 yrs	0 yrs	0 yrs	$2,500	6 months
18.2-258.2	Aiding in illegally Obtaining Prescription Drugs	Misdemeanor	12 mths	0	0	$2,500	6 months
18.2-258.2	Aiding in illegally Obtaining Prescription Drugs (2nd)	Felony	5 yrs	0 yrs	0 yrs	$2,500	6 months
18.2.260	Giving an illegal prescription not otherwise outlawed	Misdemeanor	12 mths	0	0	$2,500	6 months
18.2-248.1:1	Possession Synthetic Marijuan (Spice or K-2)	Misdemeanor	12 mths	0	0	$2,500	6 months
18.2-248.1:1	PWID Synthetic Marijuan (Spice or K-2)	Felony	5 yrs	0 yrs	0 yrs	$2,500	6 months
18.2-248.1:1	Manufacturing Synthetic Marijuan (Spice or K-2)	Felony	30 yrs	5 yrs	0 yrs	$10,000	6 months
54.1-3466	Possession of drug paraphernalia	Misdemeanor	12 mths	0	0	$2,500	NA

33

Chapter 6
What Are My Rights Before and After Arrest?

It is important for people to know their rights. It is important to know when and how to exercise those rights and what to do when they are violated.

Miranda Rights ("The police did not read me my rights.")
Miranda rights are those rights you hear in TV crime shows. The police lead away the bad guy and say, "You have the right to remain silent, anything you say or do can be used against you in a court of law…"

The police must read a suspect their Miranda rights before interrogating them in police custody if they intend to use the suspect's statements in court. If the police do not read a suspect their rights *before* interrogation, the police will not be allowed to use evidence gathered from the illegal interrogation.

Not all police interrogations involve bright lights and two-way mirrors. An interrogation occurs anytime an officer asks a question as part of an investigation. It is an interrogation even if a cop picks up a bag of weed from the sidewalk and says, "Is this yours?"

If you've been arrested and you answered any of the questions the police asked you – even "What is your name?" – tell your attorney.

Miranda rights do not apply when a suspect says something without being interrogated. If a police officer arrests a suspect and during the ride back to the station the suspect tries to explain that they are innocent because they were just holding the drugs for their friend, then that suspect just gave the officer a confession that can be used in court without reading the Miranda rights.

The police only have to read Miranda rights if an interrogation occurs in police custody. A person is in police custody is when the police limit their freedom in a significant way. Being arrested is the classic example of being in police custody. Being handcuffed, surrounded by cops, questioned in the back of a police cruiser, or while weapons are drawn may mean you are in police custody even if you are not arrested.

If you were questioned while in police custody, talk to your attorney about whether you were properly read your Miranda rights. A violation of your Miranda rights can affect the outcome of your case.

Right to Remain Silent
Never talk to police without an attorney. The most common evidence that police gather is statements by the defendant. The police don't just gather DNA evidence and finger prints, they gather words. The more words that come out of your mouth, the more likely you are to go to prison.

You're never required to talk to a police officer. You don't ever have to answer their questions and silence is rarely evidence of guilt. Don't lie. Just don't talk.

Officers are good at getting information from people who do not want to talk and they will twist your words.

For example, a cop pulls over two young men in a car and finds a bag of weed and a pipe under the back seat. He pulls the driver out of the car and says, "This is your weed and pipe isn't it?" The driver mumbles, "Yes." Then the officer says, "What other drugs do you do?" The driver responds, "Meth."

Based on the driver's confession, the officer sends the pipe to a laboratory to find microscopic amounts of meth, which he will use to charge the defendant with felony drug possession. Without that confession, the officer would have never known about the meth.

In this common example, the driver began the conversation facing a very winnable, simple marijuana possession charge, but because he said a few words lost a great defense and was also charged with felony possession of a Schedule I/II drug (meth).

I have seen this happen many times. You have an absolute right to remain silent and you should exercise that right.

If you told the police that you do not want to talk to them and they continued to ask you questions, talk to an attorney immediately. Your constitutional rights may have been violated and that may affect the outcome of your criminal case.

Right to Have an Attorney During Questioning
You have a constitutional right to have an attorney present
when you are interrogated, but only if you ask for one.

Never agree to talk to the police without an attorney, even if
you are innocent. Interrogations can be long and brutal. In
Norfolk, Virginia in 1997, detectives got four innocent men
to confess to the same brutal rape-murder after 8-12 hours of
interrogation each. When the men did not know what they
were supposed to confess too, the detective had them repeat
their confession over again until they got the details right.
Very few people can withstand an intense police
interrogation without an attorney present.

If you are not completely innocent it is even more important
to refuse to answer any questions or participate in any
interviews without your attorney. There are two good
reasons.

First, detectives will promise to help you if you help them,
but some officers or detectives may later deny that you
cooperated, or they may deny that your information was
useful or that they promised you anything. The police are
not prohibited from lying to you.

A good criminal defense attorney will know many of the
detectives; the detectives will know your attorney and the
police are much less likely to lie to you if you are
represented by an experienced attorney.

I've had several clients who cooperated with the police
before and after they hired me. In almost all of those cases

the client only got credit for the things they did *after* I was involved.

Secondly, your attorney will protect you from accidentally saying something that will result in more trouble. Anything you say can be used against you in court, but things your attorney tells the police may not be admissible in court. If you really want to talk to the police, get an attorney and you will be much safer.

If you were questioned by the police even though you asked to have an attorney, your constitutional rights may have been violated. If this happened to you, contact an attorney immediately.

Right to an Attorney at Trial
You always have a right to hire and bring your own attorney to court, but only people who are extremely poor and facing jail time are able to apply for public defenders and court appointed attorneys. The application process typically occurs at the arraignment.

If during your arraignment or trial, a judge tells you that you have a right to an attorney, this is a very strong indicator that you are in danger of going to jail. The law only requires judges to tell you about your right to an attorney if you are facing the real possibility of jail time.

Public defenders and court-appointed attorneys are not free. If you are found guilty or take any type of plea deal, you will be required to reimburse the government for the cost of your court-appointed attorney.

Making defendants pay for their court-appointed attorney when they plead guilty has led to the persistent (and false) rumor that court-appointed attorneys only get paid if their clients are found guilty.

Right to Refuse Searches

If an officer ever asks you if he can search you or your property, always say "No!" You are never required to allow a search to take place unless an officer has a search warrant or probable cause.

An officer can do anything he wants if you give him permission. However, officers cannot use intimidation or their authority as officers to force your consent to a search.

If you gave your consent to a search after the police used pressure, intimidation, or an excessive show of authority to compel your consent, talk to your attorney immediately.

If the police searched you, your property, your car or your home without your permission, talk to an attorney immediately. Illegal searches are one of the most common defenses against drug crimes.

Right Against Unreasonable Seizure

The Constitution of the United States protects all citizens from unreasonable seizure. A seizure is when the police restrain you or limit your freedom. If the police knock on your door and say, "Open up, it's the police," and you open your door, that is seizure. If a policeman pulls up and says, "Hey, you! Hands out of your pockets!" then that is a seizure.

If you are pulled over in your car, ordered out of your car, put in cuffs, told to stand still, or forced to do anything by an officer, each of those acts may constitute a seizure.

A seizure is unreasonable if the officer does not have permission, probable cause, or reasonable articulable suspicion to seize the suspect. Probable cause means there is evidence that the suspect is engaged in some criminal activity.

If you were ordered, forced, cuffed, or pulled over for no apparent reason, talk to your attorney immediately about what happened. Illegal seizures are another one of the most effective and common defenses against drug crimes.

Obstruction of Justice/Resisting Arrest
If you are being searched, seized, or arrested, you do not have to help the police, but you must not attempt to flee or take actions that impede or threaten the officers. There is a fine line between not cooperating and obstruction of justice or resisting arrest.

For example, if an officer orders you out of a car and you simply sit motionless behind a wheel until the officer jerks you out and cuffs you, you have not committed a crime in Virginia.

However, if the police tell you that you are under arrest and you take one step away, you may be charged with resisting arrest.

People often ask whether yelling or swearing at the cops is illegal. If you say anything that could be interpreted as "inciting violence," you may be charged with disorderly conduct. I always recommend that people exercise their right to remain silent.

Chapter 7
Common Illegal Stops, Searches, and Seizures

The fourth amendment to the US Constitution prevents the government from unreasonably searching or seizing its citizens.

A search is an examination of something private. It includes searching your clothes, your body, or anything that belongs to you that cannot be seen by the public. A search can be as simple as asking someone to open their hand or moving a newspaper off a car seat to what is underneath.

A seizure is when the police limit your freedom. A traffic stop is a seizure, telling someone to "freeze" is a seizure. Handcuffing or arresting a suspect is another form of seizure. Confiscating property is also a seizure.

If an officer unreasonably or illegally searches or seizes, any evidence that is found because of that search or seizure may be excluded from the trial. Arguing these two fourth amendment violations is the most common way drug cases are won.

Determining what is a reasonable search or seizure is a very complicated area of law with more exceptions than room in this book. Reading this book is never a substitute for consulting with an attorney.

However, the following examples are just some of the common ways that officers illegally search or seize suspects in drug cases. If you believe you were illegally searched or seized, or if you think one of these scenarios apply to your case, discuss it with an attorney immediately.

The Officer Stopped Me for No Reason.
Traffic stops are seizures. If an officer pulls you over, that is a seizure. If an officer pulls up to a pedestrian or a parked car and activates the cruiser's emergency light, that is usually considered a seizure as well. If an officer verbally or with hand gestures tells you to "stop" or "pull over," that is also typically a seizure.

In order to legally do this, the officer needs to have a reasonable suspicion that illegal activity or an emergency has occurred. The illegal activity can be extremely minor, such as a dead taillight, speeding, dangling objects from the rearview mirror, obscured license plate, or a blown tag light.

However minor the criminal activity, the officer must be able to articulate why he believes the illegal activity was occurring. Racial profiling, vague accusations of "suspicious activity," or driving away when the police arrive is not usually enough.

Unjustified traffic stops most often occur when the suspect is already parked or when they are walking. Many officers do not realize that pulling up and turning on their lights may be the same as a traffic stop.

I Did Not Feel Free to Refuse the Search.
An officer can search or seize you without any evidence if you willingly give them permission. Consequently, most officers will ask for permission to search whenever they

have even the slightest suspicion. Officers are not allowed to use their position and authority to force people's consent.

The Supreme Court of the United States says that a suspect's consent to search is only valid if a reasonable person in the suspect's shoes would feel free to ignore the officer's request.

Some factors that may invalidate a search or seizure include:

- Officer uses aggressive body language or tone of voice when requesting the search. (Example: Officer gets in your face and asks to search the car like he's a drill instructor.)
- Officer uses profanity or offensive language. (Example: Officer says, "Can I search the f***ing car or not?!")
- Officer repeatedly asks for permission to search. (Example: The suspect agrees to allow a search after an officer asks four or five times).
- The officer accuses you of criminal activity before asking to search. (Example: "We think you are selling drugs on this street corner, now let me see what is in your hand.")
- The officers corners or surrounds the suspect while asking permission. (Example: Three officers surround a driver who was taken out of his car on a secluded road and ask to search his car.)
- The officer threatens the suspect if they do not agree to the search. (Example: "If you don't let me search your car I am going to make you sit here for an hour

until the K-9 unit arrives." Or, "If you don't let me search you I am going to arrest you.")

- The officer asks permission while or after drawing his weapon.
- The officer touches the suspect while asking permission. (Example: The officer puts his hand on the suspect's shoulder and says, "Let me search you.")
- The officer asks permission to search after an illegal seizure. (Example: One officer illegally drags the suspect out of their car and cuffs them without justification and a second officer then comes along and politely asks for permission to search the car.)

If any of these scenarios sound similar to your case, contact an attorney immediately. You may have an important defense.

The Officer Asks for Permission to Search <u>After</u> Beginning the Search.

An officer can search or seize you without any evidence if you willingly give them permission. However, they must get your permission *before* they begin the search.

If you consented to a search, make sure you tell your attorney when you gave your consent and when the officers began the search and when they found any evidence. If the officers searched your car before asking permission, the search may have been illegal.

The Officer Asked the Wrong Person for Permission to Search.

In order to get permission to search a citizen's property, the police must ask the person who actually owns the property. Renters are treated like owners in many cases as well.

A guest of yours usually cannot give the police permission to search your private room or private storage area. A passenger normally cannot give the police permission to search another person's car. A landlord cannot give permission to search a rented apartment in many situations. A parent cannot give permission to search their adult child's private room.

If the police asked someone other than you for permission to search or seize your property, talk to an attorney immediately.

The Police's Search Went Too Far

When the police are allowed to search something, there are always limits to the scope and manner of their search.

If a person gives the police permission to search their car, the police cannot start tearing out the door panels and ripping up the carpet. This is because a reasonable person would not have interpreted giving permission to include damaging the car.

If the police are allowed to search a car, that right may not include searching bags and containers inside the car. Also, it may not include patting down the driver and passengers.

The police can go too far with search warrants as well. If a search warrant allows an officer to only search a home, the officer cannot use the search warrant to justify searching the suspect's body, pockets, or car.

When an officer justifies a search based on a probable cause or reasonable suspicion, the search must be reasonably limited to discovering evidence of the suspected illegal activity.

For example, if an officer sees a gun-shaped bulge in the waistband of a suspicious person, the officer may be allowed to stop and pat the suspect's waistband to feel if it is a gun. This suspicion alone does NOT allow the officer to then search the suspect's backpack or car.

If an officer pulls someone over for a traffic violation, the officer can detain the driver while running their driver's license and writing a ticket. But it does not mean the officer can keep the driver on the side of the road for over an hour, interrogate them about unrelated crimes, or search the car for drugs. That's going too far.

Invasive body searches, strip searches, and body cavity searches are not permitted unless an officer has very strong evidence to believe that such a search is necessary and the search is done in a way that minimizes the invasion of privacy (i.e. the officer is the same gender and the search is done in a private area out of the public's view). These types of searches are not normally allowed.

If you were searched or seized and the officers took too long, were too invasive, or went too far, then talk to an attorney immediately.

Searches or Seizures Based on a 911 Call or a Tip
The police need certain evidence to search or seize a suspect against their will. The police cannot get around this rule just because they get a tip or a phone call from a citizen or another police officer.

The US Supreme Court has said that if a police officer wants to search or seize someone because of a tip or 911 call, then the person who called the police must be 1) reliable and 2) knowledgeable.

This means the officer must have evidence that the tipster or caller is trustworthy and has also based their tip on actuals facts not just hunches. Most of the time, tips from citizens or 911 calls are not enough to justify a search or a traffic stop.

Here are some examples of illegal search and seizure that are based on tips.

- A neighbor calls 911 because two suspicious people are parked in a car along the street. The police arrive and pull up behind the parked car with their emergency lights activated. (This is illegal because the officer does not know the person calling and does not know what makes the car's occupants suspicious).
- An informant calls the police to report that he thinks two guys are selling drugs on the street corner in

front of his house. The police arrive and detain two men matching the description in front of the house. (This is illegal because the informant said nothing to the officer that would let the officer know whether his suspicions were based on facts or a mere hunch)

- An informant whom a police detective has worked with many times, tells the detective that there is an adult man sitting on a park bench with three crack rocks in a baggy in his front right pocket. The police go to the park and see three adult men and pick one to detain and search. (This search may be illegal because the police could only guess the identity of the suspect).

If the police searched or seized you based on a 911 call or tip, talk to an attorney immediately.

Police Search as a Result of an Illegal Arrest
The police can search an arrested suspect before taking them into custody. The first search occurs before the suspect is placed in the police cruiser. Another search occurs at the jail during processing.

However, if the police illegally arrest someone, the police cannot use the illegal arrest to justify the search.

For example, a suspect is arrested outside a bar for being drunk in public. The officer arrests the suspect without breathalyzing them or checking to see whether they are drunk. While searching the suspect the officer finds a bag of weed and charges the suspect with possession of marijuana.

If a judge decides that the officer did not have enough evidence to justify arresting the suspect for being drunk in public, then the arrest was illegal, the search was illegal, and the possession of marijuana case will likely be dismissed.

If you were searched as part of an arrest for another crime, talk to your attorney about the facts surrounding the officer's reasons for arresting you.

The Police Searched Something Remote as Part of the Arrest
When the police arrest a suspect, they are allowed to search the suspect and their possessions that are immediately surrounding them at the time of arrest (for example, their pockets, clothes, and any bags they are carrying with them).

A search as part of an arrest must be limited to searching the property immediately around a person at the time of arrest. An arrest search should not include bags, cars, or areas of the home not immediately around the person at the time of arrest.

A common example of a bad arrest search is when an officer arrests a person on the side of the road after getting them out of their car to talk for a few minutes, and then searches their car. The judge may decide that the car was too far away from the scene of the arrest to be included in the arrest search. The same rule applies to bags, homes, apartments, and other property.

Invasive body searches, strip searches, and body cavity searches are not permitted at the time of arrest unless an officer has very strong evidence to believe that such a search is necessary.

If the police when overboard with their arrest search, talk to an attorney immediately.

I Revoked My Permission
A person can consent to a search and then revoke their consent. If a person tells an officer that they no longer agree to the search, the officer must stop immediately unless they have enough evidence to justify a search without consent.

Typically, when people revoke their consent they often do so timidly and the police just continue to search. If you said anything during the search that suggested that you were no longer comfortable with the search, tell your attorney immediately.

The Officer Who Comes to Trial Was Not the Officer Who...
In court, a police officer usually cannot testify to things that they did not witness themselves. During many arrests, and some traffic stops, multiple officers are involved. In these situations, the officer who made first contact is usually the only one who talks to the suspect, does the searching, and makes the arrest. The other officers are supposed to aid the arresting officer only in the case of an emergency.

If multiple officers are involved in the investigation, the arresting officer may be forbidden from testifying about what the other officers heard, saw, or found. For example, if three officers search your car and one of those officers finds something, the officer who found the item is usually required to be the one who testifies to the search results. Without the correct officers present at trial, the case may be dismissed.

If any officer, other than the arresting officer, pulled you over, talked to you, participated in the search, found evidence or interacted with you, discuss it with your attorney immediately.

The Police Impounded My Car for No Reason
The police are allowed to impound a car if it is illegally parked on a public road. Typically, this happens when an officer stops a driver who is then arrested. If the car is left on public property and is not legally parked, then the police will usually tow the car.

The police are allowed to search a car they are impounding in order to inventory the contents. The purpose of this search is to make sure nothing is stolen out of the car at the impound lot. However, if the police find drugs or other evidence during the impound search, it can be used at trial.

Sometimes the police will illegally impound a car in order to search it. If any of the following situations apply to your case, your inventory search may have been illegal.

- The police searched your car before arresting you.
- The car was parked on private property (for example, private parking lots or driveways).
- The car was legally parked.
- There was a licensed driver at the scene who could have driven the car away.

If the police found evidence against you while searching your car as part of an inventory search and you believe the police illegally impounded your car, then contact an attorney immediately to discuss possible defenses.

The Police Were Trespassing Prior to the Search
Officers can search a car, home, or person if they can see, smell, or hear evidence of criminal activity. This is called the "plain view doctrine." A typical example is an officer walking down the street, looking through the window of a parked car, and seeing drugs on the seat. The officer can then enter and search the car.

However, this rule does not apply when an officer trespasses or performs an illegal search. Here are some examples of illegal searches in which the plain view doctrine does not apply.

- An officer opens a car door to get a better look inside and sees some drugs.
- An officer walks around the side of a house peeking through basement windows and sees drugs.
- An officer walks into the open garage of a house and finds drugs.
- An officer knocks on your door, talks to you in the entryway, and then steps into your house uninvited.

If the police were trespassing when they found the evidence against you, or if any of these scenarios are similar to your situation, contact an attorney to discuss any possible defenses you may have.

Miscellaneous Search Issues
There are many other ways in which the police may illegally search or seize someone. There is no substitute for talking to a criminal defense attorney who is familiar with the volumes of search and seizure cases.

In order to help your attorney defend you, make sure you tell him or her as much as you can about the following facts of your case:

- The reason the police stopped or contacted you
- Every question they asked you
- Every answer you gave them
- What they searched
- At what point they conducted the search
- What they found
- Who it was that found it
- Where it was when they found it

Chapter 8
Common Defenses to Drug Charges

The Government Can't Prove Possession
A defendant cannot be convicted for drug possession unless the government can prove that the defendant possessed the drugs.

Possession is not the same as ownership. You can possess drugs that someone else owns. If you tell the police, "Those drugs belong to my friend, I'm just holding them for him," that is a confession not a defense.

Possession means that you have some degree of physical control over the drugs. Having physical control over drugs can be as simple as holding drugs, storing drugs, moving drugs, using drugs, or touching drugs. However, having drugs in your system (being high) is not the same as possession because you no longer have any control over the drugs in your body.

Proving possession can be difficult. The police often cannot prove possession when they find drugs near a group of people (for example in a car full of people). The police may try to charge everyone in the area with possession in the hopes that one of them confesses.

However, the police must prove which member(s) of the group had physical control over the drugs. Without out some evidence of control over the drugs, the government cannot prove possession.

The Government Can't Prove that the Defendant Knew
Drugs Were Present
Possession occurs when you have physical control over
something. Possession also requires knowledge. To possess
drugs you must know that the drugs are present.

Being the driver or owner of the car is not enough to prove
possession of drugs found in a car. The government must be
able to prove that the defendant knew the drugs were
present. The same rule that applies to cars can apply to
homes, bags, and other property. If the drugs were not in
plain sight or in your pants pocket, the police will probably
be required to prove you knew the drugs were present.

The police will try to prove possession by getting the
defendant to admit that they knew the drugs were present.
That is why remaining silent and talking to your attorney
about all conversations with the police is so important.

The Government Can't Prove the Defendant Knew the
Substance was Drugs
To prove that a defendant possessed drugs, the government
must prove that the defendant knew the substance was
marijuana, cocaine, or some other illegal drug.

This can be difficult when the possession charge is based on
resin, residue, or trace amounts of drugs. For example, if an
officer searches the floor of a car and finds a discarded
baggie with one or two flecks of marijuana inside, the
government will have to prove that the defendant knew
those green flecks were marijuana.

In cases involving synthetic marijuana or prescription drugs containing controlled substances, the police may be required to prove that the person knew that those drugs contained an illegal substance. This can be extremely difficult to prove without a confession by the suspect.

In such cases, the police question suspects and try to get confessions. Always exercise your right to remain silent and tell your attorney everything you said to the police.

Government Cannot Prove Distribution
Possession with intent to distribute (PWID) is much more serious than simple possession. To prove PWID, the government must prove that the defendant possessed drugs and intended to distribute those drugs.

The government will try to use the defendant's text messages and admissions, confidential informants, and undercover detectives to prove PWID.

The police will also try to use circumstantial evidence, such as scales, multiple small packages of drugs, large quantities of drugs, or large amounts of cash on the suspect. This type of evidence alone may not be enough to prove PWID. If your arrest for PWID is based on circumstantial evidence, discuss it with your attorney immediately.

The Government Can't Prove the Weight of the Drugs
For many PWID cases and some possession cases, the weight of the drugs found on the defendant has a major effect on the outcome of the case. For example, PWID

marijuana of more than .5 ounces is a felony, whereas less than .5 ounces is a misdemeanor.

In situations where the weight of the drugs may lead to elevated punishments, it is important that the government prove the exact weight of the drugs.

However, when weighing drugs that are mixed (or "cut") with other substances, the weight of the entire substance, including impurities, is counted towards any enhanced punishments. For example, if a suspect is arrested for PWID cocaine mixed with baking soda, the combined weight of the baking soda and cocaine is used for sentencing. The defendant cannot avoid the enhanced punishment by claiming that only part of the weight was actually cocaine.

Often the police will attempt to weigh the drugs while they're still inside their packaging, which can sometimes add significant weight to the measurement.

When the drugs are measured, the quality and calibration of the scale may come into question and the person who measured the drugs may be forced to appear in court for cross-examination by your attorney. If the person or techniques used to weigh the drugs do not stand up to cross-examination, or if the person who did the weighing fails to appear in court, the weight of the drugs may be excluded from evidence.

The Government Can't Prove a Miscellaneous Element of the Crime

Several drug crimes include miscellaneous elements. Some examples could include: the defendant's proximity to a school at the time of possession, whether a BB gun found on the defendant counts as a firearm, and whether a prescription the defendant used was forged.

The government has to prove all elements of the crime beyond a reasonable doubt. When talking to your attorney it is important to discuss each element of the crime and whether or not the government can prove each one.

Illegal Search

Evidence produced by an illegal search cannot be used at a trial. In most drug cases, an illegal search results in the dismissal of the entire charge. It is important to understand your rights in order to communicate effectively with your attorney.

If the police searched you or your property, read the chapter on illegal searches and seizures and discuss your search in detail with your attorney.

Illegal Stop/Seizure

A seizure is when the police restrict your freedom. Some examples of seizures include: being pulled over, being arrested, being handcuffed, being ordered to do something, or having the police take control of your possessions.

Every drug case involves at least one seizure by the police. You and your attorney should discuss and identify each seizure and its constitutionality. If a drug case is based on an illegal seizure, the case may be dismissed entirely.

To learn more about illegal seizures, read the chapter on illegal searches and seizures and discuss it with your attorney.

Illegal Arrest
An officer must have sufficient evidence that a suspect committed a crime before arresting them. The police cannot justify the arrest with evidence they find after the arrest,

When talking with your attorney, make sure you clearly communicate the point at which each piece of evidence was found and the point at which you were arrested.

Illegal arrests happen most frequently when a person is arrested for a very minor nuisance crime (for example, being drunk in public or disorderly conduct). When an officer arrests someone for these types of offenses, the officer is often only concerned with getting the person off the street. The officer may not care whether the minor charge actually results in a conviction so they may be sloppy about whether or not the arrest is valid.

However, as the person is being arrested and searched, the officer may find drugs and then charge the person with the additional drug crimes. If the defense attorney can show that the initial arrest was invalid, then both charges will be dismissed.

If your drug charge stems from an arrest for another charge, discuss that other charge in all of its detail, because it may be very important to your drug case.

No Laboratory Drug Test
The government must prove beyond a reasonable doubt that the substance in question was not only a drug, but the specific type of drug as well. This usually requires a drug test.

There are two basic types of law enforcement drug tests. There are the field test kits that the police on the street use to justify a drug arrest. And there are the tests run by the Department of Forensic Science (DFS) laboratory which are used to convict defendants of drug charges.

For most drug cases the field test kits are not reliable enough to justify convicting someone. The government must have a DFS certificate of analysis which states the exact type of drug and the quantity.

The one exception to this rule is simple possession of marijuana. The government can convict someone of simple possession of marijuana without a DFS laboratory test only if the officer or the government notifies the defendant of their right to request a DFS lab test.

If the government fails to notify the defendant of their right to get an independent DFS lab test, the government may not be allowed to use the marijuana field test kits as evidence at trial. If you are charged with possession of marijuana, discuss with your attorney whether or not you received any paperwork regarding your right to get the marijuana tested.

An Invalid Certificate of Drug Analysis
The US Supreme Court case Melendez-Diaz v. Massachusetts changed drug prosecution in the United States. The Melendez-Diaz ruling states that a defendant has a constitutional right to cross-examine technicians who perform drug tests in police laboratories.

If a defendant is not given an opportunity to cross examine these witnesses, then the court may determine that the lab test is not admissible evidence.

Excluding the laboratory certificate of analysis in a drug case may result in a dismissal.

In Virginia, a prosecutor may attempt to restrict your Melendez-Diaz rights. A competent criminal defense attorney can easily prevent this from happening by filing a notice with the court within a very specific time period. Make sure you hire a criminal defense attorney as soon as possible so that your attorney has enough time to file this paperwork.

Invalid Drug Test Kit
Police can only use a valid drug test kit. To be valid, the make and model of the kit must be approved by the Department of Forensic Science (DFS).

Also, the kit must be used properly and before its expiration date.

The Marijuana Stalks Were Mature
Mature marijuana stalks have very little THC and no real recreational value but can be used for legal purposes. Consequently, mature marijuana stalks are not considered marijuana under Virginia law.

If the marijuana found on a defendant is residue, ash, or indeterminate plant material, the government may not be able to determine whether it is from the stalk of a mature marijuana plant. Drug testing will only determine whether the material contains any measurable amount of THC, and residue from mature stalks can also test positive for THC.

The Officer was Outside His Jurisdiction
A county or local police officer can only act as a police officer inside his own jurisdiction.

Make sure you know what type of police officer pulled you over, stopped you, and arrested you (county, state, federal, city/town, college police, metro police, or park police). If you were stopped, chased, or arrested outside the officer's jurisdiction tell your attorney immediately.

College or university police officers have jurisdiction on campus property and on roads abutting campus property. The Washington Metropolitan Airport Authority Police have authority at Dulles and Reagan National airports and along some of the access roads (such as the Dulles toll road).

County, city, and town officers generally can enforce the law 300 yards outside of their jurisdiction. They can also chase a person up to a mile outside their jurisdiction.

Multiple Officers Involved In Your Case

During an investigation, traffic stop, search, or arrest, there are usually several officers on the scene. However, only one officer should be interacting with the suspect.

The first officer on the scene should take charge as the arresting officer while the others should be there only as back-up in case of emergency.

The reason for this rule is simple. An officer can only testify to what he personally witnesses, not to what someone else witnesses. If multiple officers are involved in the investigation, then more than one officer may be required to show up at trial.

Each officer is scheduled to appear in court on a dedicated court date. It can become a logistical nightmare if multiple officers are required on your case. This can be a major strategic advantage for the defense, but only if the defense attorney is aware of the situation.

If someone other than the arresting officer stopped you, searched you or your property, found evidence, questioned you, or otherwise interacted with you, talk to your attorney immediately. Make sure your attorney knows which officers did what.

Wrong Court (Wrong Jurisdiction)

Before a court can pass judgment on you, it must have jurisdictional authority. General District Court has no authority over minors, and Prince William County courts have no authority over cases that occurred in Arlington. The

Federal courts cannot hear state law cases that occurred outside of federal jurisdictions. Make sure your attorney knows where each aspect of your case occurred and what court you have been summoned to appear in.

Invalid Warrantless Arrest
Under Virginia law, a police officer is allowed to arrest a person for a misdemeanor without a warrant only when the officer witnesses the crime or under very specific circumstances.

Those circumstances include: the scene of a car accident on a public road, at the hospital after a car accident, in shoplifting cases, in DUI cases (within three hours of driving), and a few other situations.

Your arrest may have been invalid IF:

- You were arrested for a misdemeanor
- The police officer did not have an arrest warrant
- The officer did not witness you commit the crime and
- You were not at the scene of a motor vehicle accident on a public road, transported to the hospital after an accident, shoplifting or drunk driving within three hours of the arrest.

Pre-Sentencing Report and Sentencing Guideline Errors
Figuring out what punishment to give a person can be much more complicated than determining whether they are guilty. The Pre-Sentencing Report and Virginia Sentencing

Guidelines are prepared by probation officers and used by judges when sentencing the defendant.

The Pre-Sentencing Report is 20 to 40 pages. The probation officer will interview the defendant before the sentencing hearing to gather information for the report.

The probation officer will ask the defendant their version of events, their background, their employment, and their substance abuse history, among other things.

A favorable and accurate Pre-Sentencing Report can be extremely beneficial. The defendant should be prepared for the interview and review the final report with their attorney prior to the sentencing hearing. Many of these reports contain errors which should be clarified before the sentencing hearing.

The Virginia Sentencing Guidelines are a complex series of mathematical formulas and charts that determine a defendant's recommended punishment. This formula is calculated by the probation officer and included in the Pre-Sentencing Report.

Past criminal history, number of counts, whether a weapon was involved, juvenile record, whether the defendant has served jail time, the amount of drugs, and the defendant's probation status at the time of the offense are all examples of factors that affect the sentencing recommendation.

It is very common for the sentencing recommendation to be calculated wrong. These errors can be caused by flawed criminal background checks, inaccurate court records, human error, or vagueness in the guidelines themselves.

These errors can be the difference between no jail time and years in jail. Your attorney must know everything about your adult and juvenile criminal record whether it happened in Virginia or outside Virginia. Your attorney must also be well versed and trained in calculating the Virginia Sentencing Guidelines. Always review your Pre-Sentencing Report and your Sentencing Guidelines with your attorney prior to your sentencing hearing.

The 251 Program (First Offender Program)
Va. Code 18.2-251 states that the courts may place first-time drug offenders in a special program called the "251 program." If the defendant successfully completes the drug program the case may be dismissed.

The 251 program differs slightly from locality to locality, but it typically involves all of the following:

- 6 to 12 months of probation
- Fines, court costs, and fees
- 100 percent abstinence from drugs and alcohol
- Passing drugs and alcohol tests
- 24 hours of community service
- A six-month license suspension
- 10 weeks or more of ASAP classes.

Even though successful completion will result in dismissal, there are some hidden downsides to the 251 program.

Completing the 251 program does NOT mean the criminal record is sealed or hidden. When you are arrested for any criminal offense, a record of your arrest is made. Likewise, the results of the criminal case are also recorded.

If you plead guilty and complete the 251 program your records will indicate that you pled guilty, completed a program, and the case was dismissed. Most if not all of this basic information will be public.

You cannot get an expungement or seal your record if you plead guilty or enter the 251 program.

Another problem with the 251 program is that you still lose your driver's license for six months. Talk to your attorney to determine whether a restricted license may be available.

If you are not a US citizen, the immigration consequences of completing the 251 program and being convicted are exactly the same. Most drug crimes, including simple possession of marijuana, will likely result in deportation.

If you are on probation or parole, entering the 251 program may result in a probation violation. If you are on any type of probation or parole you must talk to an attorney about it before deciding to enter any programs. A 251-dismissal may still land you in jail.

Not everyone can successfully complete the 251 program. If there is any doubt as to whether you can successfully pass all the drugs test, complete the courses, and stay out of legal trouble for the entire probation period, you should discuss these problems with your attorney. Do not get set up for failure.

Your attorney may be able to arrange a plea to another offense (such as possession of paraphernalia) that does not involve a loss of license, ASAP classes, probation, or drug testing.

Even felony drug possession charges may be dismissed via a 18.2-251 disposition if the judge is willing to allow it. Getting a 251 disposition for felony drug possession is much more discretionary and not necessarily allowed as a matter of right.

An experienced criminal defense attorney can give you counsel on how to obtain a 251 disposition for a drug possession charge and whether a 251 disposition is right for you.

For more information on the 251 program read Chapter 9.

The Do-It-Yourself 251 Program
There are many reasons why a first offender program or "251 program" may be unacceptable to a defendant charged with simple possession of marijuana: the six-month loss of license, the immigration consequences, or the effects on education, security clearance, or employment.

One alternative may be an unofficial or "do-it-yourself" 251 program.

In this scenario, defendants put themselves through something very similar to the 251 program prior to their court date. They abstain from all drugs and alcohol, they do 25 hours of community service, they go through drug and alcohol testing, and they may even sign up for ASAP or a similar program.

After completing all of these difficult and time-consuming tasks, the defense attorney presents this to the prosecution in an attempt to get the prosecution to dismiss the charges. If the prosecution dismisses the charges, there is no record of conviction at all.

Unlike the official 251 program, the do-it-yourself version will not trigger deportation, security clearance violations, or in any way appear on your record as a conviction. Neither will it result in a six-month loss of license.

Of course, this strategy has no guarantees. After all of that hard work, the prosecutor may refuse to agree to dismiss the charge. If the defendant then has to go through the regular 251 program, their pre-trial community service hours and drug testing efforts cannot be applied to the regular 251 program requirements.

This defense strategy takes a lot of time and it is not a good fit for everyone. There is no substitute for consulting a criminal defense attorney as soon as possible.

Chapter 9
Virginia's First Offender Diversion Program (18.2-251)

The vast majority of drug charges are for simple possession by a first-time offender. Most of those possession charges involve marijuana. Many of those defendants will be asked by a judge whether or not they want to enroll in the "251 program.".

The 251 program allows a defendant to have a first-time drug possession charge dismissed so long as they comply with a lengthy and strict set of conditions. While having charges dismissed sounds great, there are many conditions and exceptions attached to the 251 program.

251 Program Requirements
A defendant who enters the 251 program must plead guilty or stipulate that the evidence is sufficient for a finding of guilt by the court. This means that even though your charge may be dismissed later on, entering the 251 program will affect your immigration status if you are not a US citizen and will likely result in deportation despite successful completion of the program. This also disqualifies 251 participants from getting an expungement.

Some employers, educational institutions, and security clearance providers consider a 251 dismissal the same a conviction because it requires a defendant to plead guilty. If you are concerned about the effects of a conviction on your work, security clearance, or schooling opportunities, then talk to an attorney immediately.

The 251 program also requires the defendant to acknowledge that any violation of the probationary terms and conditions is grounds for a finding of guilt by the court. So if a defendant enters the 251 program and then violates the terms of probation, they will not have a chance to fight the charges. Once a defendant enters the program, they must complete the program or they will be convicted and punished.

Defendants who enter the 251 program agree to allow the proceedings to be deferred and to be placed on active probation with the county Alcohol Safety Action Program for six months followed by another six months of inactive probation.

The terms of the active probation include 10 weeks (two hours a week) of classes but can also include more intensive counseling and even rehab if ASAP determines that such treatment is necessary.

Admission to the 251 program also requires that a defendant keep the court notified if their address changes while on probation. Failure to update your address can cause serious legal problems.

251 program attendees agree that any notice of probation violations can simply be mailed to the address on file as opposed to being served by a sheriff's deputy.

If a defendant violates their probation, the court can then either fix a time for the defendant to become compliant or set a time for the defendant to be found guilty of possession for non-compliance.

"251" First Offender Program Requirements

- Plead guilty (this can cause immigration problems)
- Be placed on active probation with ASAP
- Pay $350 for ASAP plus court costs and other fees
- Complete the 10-week ASAP program on time
- Pass drug tests during probation
- No drugs or alcohol while on probation
- Suspended driver's license for six months
- Complete 24 hours of community service

Costs and Fees for the First Offender Program
(All dollar amounts in this chapter are estimates and are subject to constant change. Please use these amounts as estimates only)

251 participants are responsible for all costs, including drug screening, drug testing, and treatment (unless they can show the court they are indigent).

The cost of participating in the 251 program is $350, which includes your initial assessment at ASAP, education classes, probation monitoring, and drug screenings. (Fairfax County ASAP won't take cash but will accept check, credit card, or money order).

The $350 cost includes the following:

- $150 for the intake assessment and probation supervision
- $100 for the education intervention
- Two urine screens valued at $50 each

These costs are in addition to the court costs and fines that the court may also impose.

A defendant must pay extra if they're referred to counseling or treatment in addition to the 10-week course. Extra treatment is more likely for defendants who have any type of substance abuse problem.

These extra classes and treatment can cost a few hundred dollars or even thousands. Extra treatment can include mandatory inpatient rehab in extreme cases.

Defendants who are required to do community service will have to pay a fee to the service organization as well.

If you miss an ASAP class or appointment or even run late, your mere tardiness will cost you a $25 "processing fee." Tardiness can also result in a probation violation and expulsion from the program.

Failure to pay any of these fees, fines, or costs can result in incompletion of the program and a violation of probation.

Conditions of Probation
As part of the ASAP program, all defendants must agree to remain drug and alcohol free for six to 12 months. They must also agree to submit to drug and alcohol tests by ASAP. Anyone who admits using drugs or alcohol or who shows up to ASAP classes exhibiting signs of drug or alcohol use will be required to submit to extra tests.

A copy of the 2011 Fairfax County General District Court ASAP order form for drug possession charges is included in this section as a reference. Similar order forms exist for each jurisdiction's ASAP program.

Defendants who enter the 251 program will be required to complete 24 hours of approved community service and make a reasonable effort to get and keep a job.

If a defendant fails to comply with any of the terms of their 251 probation they can be found guilty of their original charge and punished without an opportunity for a trial.

Six-Month Driver's License Suspension
Defendants who enter the 251 program will lose their driver's license for six months if they have a Virginia driver's license. However, Virginia drivers can ask the judge for a restricted license allowing them limited driving to and from work, school, church, medical appointments, ASAP, and a few other possible exceptions. Talk to your attorney about your driving needs and work schedule to find out whether a restricted licensed would be possible or practical.

IN THE FAIRFAX COUNTY GENERAL DISTRICT COURT

ORDER INTO ASAP FOR DRUG POSSESSION CHARGES

COMMONWEALTH OF VIRGINIA)
COUNTY OF FAIRFAX/CITY OF FAIRFAX)
      VS)   Criminal Case No. _____
)
_____)

Defendant's Agreement:

1. The above named defendant has pled guilty or has stipulated that the evidence is sufficient for a finding of guilt by the Court pursuant to §18.2-251 of the Code of Virginia; and,

2. The defendant acknowledges that any violation of this Order is grounds for a finding of guilt by the Court based upon said plea or evidence; and

3. The defendant consents that further proceedings be deferred and that he be placed on probation with the Fairfax County Alcohol Safety Action Program (ASAP) according to the terms and conditions of the probation agreement, including an evaluation for treatment and/or education as may be best suited to the needs of the defendant.

4. The defendant verifies that the mailing address listed on the warrant or summons is his correct mailing address and the defendant agrees to notify the Court and Fairfax ASAP of any address changes during the period of probation; and

5. The defendant agrees that any notice of non-compliance with the terms and conditions of this Order may be made by sending notice by first class mail to the address of record, specifying any violation and setting forth a date by which compliance is to be met or placing the case on the docket to recommend a finding of guilt to the Court; and

Terms and Conditions:

1. The defendant shall pay all court costs and all or part of the costs of the program, including for screening, testing and treatment, based upon the defendant's ability to pay unless he is determined by the Court to be indigent; and

2. The defendant shall be fingerprinted as a condition of referral to the ASAP Program; and

3. The defendant shall remain drug and alcohol free during the period of probation and submit to such tests during that period as may be necessary and appropriate to determine if the defendant is drug free; and

4. The defendant shall perform **24 HOURS** of community service as prescribed by statute, successfully complete the required treatment and/or education program, and make a reasonable effort to secure and/or maintain employment.

5. Defendant's driver's license shall be suspended for a period of six months, as required by Code, and a restricted license issued, if approved by a judge.

Order:

1. IT IS HEREBY ORDERED that this cause be continued until_____, at which time the Court shall dismiss the proceedings and discharge the defendant if all agreements, terms and conditions as set forth herein are fulfilled; and

2. Fairfax ASAP shall report to this court regarding the defendant's participation and including a record check to confirm no further violations of law; and

3. The defendant need not appear for dismissal unless noticed as set forth in # 4 above or ordered by the Court to appear.

SEEN AND AGREED:

_____   _____
DEFENDANT   JUDGE

_____   _____
ATTORNEY FOR DEFENDANT   DATE

Drivers with non-Virginia driver's licenses will be banned from driving in Virginia but the Virginia courts do not have the authority to suspend their right to drive outside of Virginia. Out-of-state drivers are not often given restricted licenses by most judges. Out-of-state drivers' home states can also choose to suspend their right to drive outside of Virginia.

ASAP Eligibility Requirements
To be eligible for the 251 program a defendant must have no prior record of drug offenses, concurrent drug charges, or a 18.2-251 disposition.

However, just because you may have a prior record does not necessarily mean that the ASAP program will have evidence of it. This is more likely if your prior charge occurred in a remote jurisdiction, when you were a minor, or before a name change due to marriage.

You are eligible for the 251 program unless ASAP says you are not eligible, and even then you may be able to get into the program with the assistance of a knowledgeable criminal defense attorney.

All 251 program participants must be able to complete the program in six to 12 months as a condition of eligibility.

Effects of the 251 Program on Criminal Record and Immigration Status
If a defendant successfully completes the 251 program, their criminal record will show that their crime was dismissed due to successful completion of the 251 program. A defendant cannot expunge or "seal" the record of their 251 dismissal in Virginia at this time.

If you have a 251 dismissal on your criminal record, law enforcement and other people who look at your complete criminal record will be able to tell that your dismissal was part of the 251 program and not because you were found "not guilty." In the eyes of some people, a 251 dismissal is not the same as a true dismissal.

A dismissal through the 251 program has the same effect on one's immigration status as a conviction. If you are not a US citizen, a conviction for almost any drug offense (including the lowest form of marijuana possession) can result in deportation. If you are not a US citizen, hire an attorney immediately upon your arrest for any drug crime.

Indicators that the 251 Program May Not Be a Good Idea for Your Case.
Entering the 251 program instead of fighting your charge may not be a good idea IF:

- *You are not guilty or have good legal defenses.* Why go through the 251 program if you are not guilty or if the government has no case? Always consult a competent attorney before agreeing to enter the 251 program.
- *You cannot afford to lose your driver's license for six months.* Entering the 251 program will result in a six-month loss of driving privileges. Restricted licenses are not always available. If this is unacceptable, talk to an attorney before entering the 251 program.
- *You may get another drug charge in the future.* Most officers, prosecutors, and judges treat a 251 dismissal on your record the same as a conviction. Suspects with a 251 dismissal on their records are less likely to be cut a

break by an officer on the street or by a prosecutor or judge.

- *You may want to do the 251 program in the future.* Preserve your ability to go through the 251 program if at all possible as a form of insurance against potential future charges.
- *You cannot 100 percent abstain from all illegal drugs and alcohol.* Defendants in the 251 program will undergo drug and alcohol testing. If you fail these tests you can violate your probation. If you are not 100 percent confident in your ability to stay clean, the 251 program may not be a good idea.
- *You are not a US citizen.* The 251 program can result in your deportation if you are not a US citizen. Talk to an attorney immediately if you are ever charged with a drug crime.
- *You are on probation.* Because entering the 251 program involves admitting that the facts are sufficient to find you guilty, doing so may cause you to violate your probation. Consult an attorney immediately if you were on probation when you were charged with drug possession.
- *You want your day in court.* You have a constitutional right to a trial. Do not give up that right without a good reason.

Chapter 10
Working With the Police as a Confidential Informant

Many people who are arrested for serious drug crimes are approached by detectives wanting information. Those detectives may or may not make vague promises of assistance. If you are approached by the police for information about criminal activity, immediately tell your attorney, whether you intend to cooperate or not.

If you are considering talking to the police in exchange for assistance, or if you have information regarding serious criminal activity, you need to talk to an experienced criminal defense attorney immediately.

Working with the police can bring wonderful results. It can also be an utter disaster if done wrong. A competent attorney can:

- Make sure that the police hold up their end of the bargain
- Protect your identity
- Protect you from incriminating yourself in additional crimes
- Coach and assist you
- Help you get results that will make a difference

What Benefits Can I Expect From Cooperating With Police?
Giving information to the police is not a magic wand. There are very few detectives or prosecutors who will make any concrete promises regarding deals.

However, a rule of thumb is that the prosecution will dismiss one of your charges if you help them get at least two other arrests of equivalent seriousness. For example, if you are arrested for PWID cocaine (25 grams) you would normally have to help the police get two felony PWID arrests for hard drugs of approximately the same quantity to get the charges dropped. Those two arrests can be for the same person or two different people.

Because the police and prosecution will not make any promises, it is vitally important that you have an attorney that has an excellent working relationship with detectives and the prosecution. That relationship is what will protect an informant from being betrayed by the police or prosecution.

Have Your Attorney Present
Cooperating with the police makes a big difference in your case but only if it is done right. Always have your attorney present if and when you ever talk to the police.

Having your attorney present is important because your attorney can prevent you from saying something that could hurt you. Your attorney can also help guarantee that the police hold up their end of the bargain.

What Do I Have to Do?
If you decide to cooperate with the police, the first thing that will happen is an interview. The informant, the detectives, and the defense attorney will all sit down and the informant will tell the police what he knows. Typically, the detectives will have lists of names and phone numbers from your phone if it was confiscated.

If the police like what they hear, they will want to arrange for the informant to buy drugs. If you are on probation, you may not be allowed to participate in a drug buy.

Sometimes informants arrange for an undercover detective to buy drugs from a suspect. Sometimes the informant will buy drugs themselves. Sometimes an informant will simply inform the detective when a suspect has the drugs in their car or house so the police can raid them. The police may do a combination of these things as well.

For more serious cases the police will often have the informant make several transactions before they arrest a suspect. The arrest may occur minutes or days after the arranged drug buy.

Most stings are arranged so that the suspect does not know who set them up and so that the informant does not have to testify in court. This is done to protect the informant and to prevent the prosecution from having to rely on an informant in order to get a conviction.

Talking with Detectives
The informant should avoid talking about things that they have done or the details surrounding their immediate case. Instead, the conversation should be focused on what other people are doing. If the conversation strays to talking about the informant, the attorney can interrupt. If an informant is ever nervous or has question they will usually be allowed to stop and privately consult with their attorney.

In some jurisdictions, the prosecution will offer an official immunity letter that guarantees protection from prosecution for crimes confessed during a confidential interview. In jurisdictions where immunity letters are used, they will often not guarantee immunity from violent crimes.

The interview will go more smoothly if the informant and his attorney discuss what they will talk about prior to meeting with the detectives.

What Crimes do Detectives Care the Most About?
Not all information has the same value. The police give bigger rewards for information that leads to bigger convictions. While any information may be useful, the following is a list of the top 10 drug crimes that narcotics detectives really want information about.

1. Shipping drugs through the mail.
2. Carrying a weapon while dealing or possessing.
3. Manufacturing drugs (Meth, GHB, etc.)
4. Transporting more than .5 ounces across state lines
5. Growing marijuana
6. Prescription forgery or fraud scams
7. Prescription drug arrangements with corrupt doctors or pharmacists
8. Large-quantity dealers
9. Dealers of heroin and other hard drugs (cocaine, crack, mali, ecstasy, etc.)
10. Gang or organized crime drug activity

Information about any criminal activity is important, but typically narcotics detectives care most about narcotics crimes in their own jurisdictions.

What Kind of Information Do the Detectives Want?
The worst thing you can do is show up to a meeting with detectives and then waste their time. The detective's opinion of how helpful you have been can have a huge effect on your case.

Talk with your attorney prior to the meeting and share what information you have. You attorney will be able to help coach you and will be able to keep a record of the information you gave so that detectives cannot later claim you did not help.

Your attorney can also help you communicate more effectively by making sure you are prepared with the appropriate hard facts and information.

Here is a list of the types of information you may want to provide.

1. Full names (not just nicknames)
2. Home address, work location, telephone number, and the kind of car they drive (make, model & color)
3. Types of drugs they use or deal
4. Quantities that they use or deal.
5. How often they "re-up" or renew their stock of drugs
6. Locations where each person deals
7. Locations where they store their drugs

8. Names of their friends, customers, and family members
9. Whether or not you think you could get them to sell you drugs or whether you know someone they would sell to
10. Whether or not they are involved in bigger crimes (have a weapon, transport across state lines, ship drugs in the mail, manufacture or grow drugs, etc.).

Before you meet with detectives, go through your information with your attorney. If you don't know someone's address, full name, or other information, then try to find out prior to the meeting.

The more complete your information, the more impressed the detectives will be and the more likely it will result in a favorable outcome for your case.

Coordinating With the Police
If the police like your information, they will want to use you to arrange drug purchases. Arranging a drug buy can take weeks or months and can take many attempts before it succeeds.

Not only do you have to arrange a purchase but you must do it when you, the police, and the suspect are all available. If you want your cooperation to help your pending case, you have to achieve results before your trial. If you wait until the last minute you will probably fail.

When cooperating with the police, the detectives expect you to return their phone calls quickly. When the detectives are ready to do a drug buy, they expect you to drop what you were doing and help them immediately. The detectives will not usually return these courtesies because they are not facing criminal charges.

If you decide to cooperate with the police, be prepared to help on their terms, when they ask for it, and not the other way around.

If the police are slow using your services, talk to your attorney. If the police are being difficult or rude to you then talk to your attorney. Your attorney can do a lot to smooth things over.

Is Cooperating with the Police Dangerous?
Cooperating with the police is extremely common. Every day dozens of people are working with the police as part of a plea deal or for money.

Normally, defendants who become informants are not present during an arrest and they normally do not have to testify in court. Often, the suspect does not even know who set them up. For the vast majority of defendants, giving the police information is safe when done with their attorney present.

However, if you believe that a specific group or certain individuals pose a serious threat to your or your family's safety, discuss it with your attorney. There are several things that your attorney can do to increase your safety.

Chapter 11
Bail, Bond, and Pre-Trial Supervision

What is a Magistrate?

A magistrate is similar to a judge. A Magistrate issues arrest warrants and is the first person to make a decision regarding your bond.

When a person is arrested and taken to jail, they are brought before a magistrate. The arresting officer tells his version of the events and gives a copy of the defendant's criminal record to the magistrate.

The magistrate then decides whether to set a bond and how much the bond should be.

A bond is collateral, used to guarantee that a defendant shows up to court and stays out of trouble pending their trial.

There are five types of bond status:

1. Recognizance (or a summons). Recognizance means you are released with nothing more than your promise to show up to court and to stay out of trouble. When you are issued a summons you are released on recognizance.

2. Unsecured bond. An unsecured bond is a bond you don't pay unless you get into trouble or don't show up. For example, if a magistrate gives you an $8,000 unsecured bond, it means that you are released from jail pending your trial, but if you do not show up to court or you get in trouble, then you will owe the court $8,000.

3. *Secured bond*. Secured bonds must be paid before you are released from jail. The court will return the money paid only if you complete your trial without violating the terms of your bond. Bail bondsman will pay secured bonds for you in exchange for a fee (typically 10 percent).

4. *No bond*. Sometimes the magistrate will refuse to allow you to be released from jail pending trial. The magistrate often does this when the crime is particularly serious, the defendant has a bad criminal record, the defendant is a flight risk, or if the defendant has an ICE detainer (they are being deported).

5. *Pre-trial Supervision*. The court can order a person to participate in pre-trial services as a condition of bond. Pre-trial services assign you a probation officer. You complete drug tests, check in with a probation officer (PO), and/or do whatever your PO tells you to do. Pre-trial supervision is an alternative to no bond or an expensive secured bond.

Terms and Condition of Bond
A bond, whether secured or unsecured, always comes with conditions. All bonds contain the promise that you'll appear at your trial and not break the law. However, some bonds include special conditions, such as:

- Protective orders against victims
- Not being allowed to leave the state
- Ankle bracelets with GPS locators
- Abstinence from drugs and alcohol

- SCRAM ankle bracelets which test your sweat for the presence of alcohol.

Most bail bondsman can help with the logistics of getting GPS or SCRAM ankle bracelets fitted. Your attorney can also answer questions regarding the conditions of your bond and what you can do to amend the terms of your bond.

Appealing a Magistrate's Decision
If the magistrate does not give you a bond, or if the magistrate sets a high or restrictive bond, you can appeal that decision. Magistrates' decisions are appealed to JDR or GDC. GDC and JDR decisions are appealed to Circuit Court.

Bond motions or bond appeals don't take long to process – usually about one business day. At the bond motion, the judge's two biggest concerns are whether the defendant is a flight risk and whether the defendant is a danger to the community.

In determining whether a person is a flight risk or a danger, the judge will look at the following factors:

- Whether the underlying charge is one that creates a presumption against bond (rape, murder, and other specific crimes)
- Length and seriousness of prior criminal record
- Prior convictions for failure to appear in court (FTA); probation violations; violation of a protective order; fugitive from justice; eluding, or resisting arrest
- The nature and seriousness of the underlying charge

- Whether there are victims who would be afraid or in danger if the defendant was released
- Whether a firearm was used
- The defendant's ties to the community (family, job, property ownership, etc.)
- Length of residence and ties to the community
- Whether the defendant is likely to try to obstruct justice
- Whether the defendant has other pending charges
- Whether the defendant has a fixed address in the jurisdiction
- Whether the defendant is an illegal immigrant, deportable, or has an ICE detainer
- The defendant's financial resources
- Whether defendant's children, family, or employees will be negatively affected by holding the defendant in jail
- Any other relevant factors

Why Was I Not Given a Bond?

Some situations commonly result in being held without bond. An appeal may change this. If the following factors apply to the defendant, it may be more difficult to get them out on bond.

1) Charged with an act of violence
2) Charged with a certain type of sexual assault
3) Committed a felony while on probation, bond, or pretrial release
4) Multiple recent prior drug charges
5) Charged with transporting drugs into Virginia
6) Charged with PWID near a school, park, etc.

7) Charged with distributing drugs to minors
8) Charged with possession of a firearm on school property
9) Is not a US citizen or has an ICE detainer
10) Is in jail on a probation violation
11) Has a prior Failure to Appear conviction

If you or someone you love is held without bond or is on a very high bond, contact an attorney immediately to discuss a bond motion.

How Can I Contact Someone Who is Held In Jail?
Most jails will allow attorneys to call inmates, and some jails will allow inmates to call registered attorneys for free.

Some jails allow inmates to make collect calls. Other jails allow inmates to make calls if they have money in their phone accounts.

Calls to and from the jail are recorded and can be used by the prosecution at the trial. Never discuss an inmate's case over the phone! Some jails provide non-recorded and confidential phone lines for attorneys to call their clients.

All jails allow attorneys to visit inmates, but this can be a very time consuming process for an attorney.

Family members can arrange visitation through the sheriff's department. Each jail has different rules, times, and procedures for depositing funds, dropping off medications, or sending letters.

ICE Detainers, Transportation Orders and Detainers Generally

A detainer is when another branch of the government or law enforcement requests custody of an inmate. It's a way of calling "dibs" on an inmate.

Once an inmate with a detainer is ready for release, the jail holds the inmate until the department that placed the detainer picks up the inmate.

ICE detainers are detainers issued by the Department of Homeland Security's (DHS) Immigration and Customs Enforcement (ICE). If an inmate is a deportable alien or an undocumented alien, ICE may choose to issue a detainer.

Most jails in Virginia have a staff person who is supposed to check the immigration status of all inmates and notify ICE if they find a deportable immigrant.

If a loved one is an illegal or deportable alien and is arrested, do everything possible to get them out on bond before the ICE representatives issue a detainer. Getting out on bond very quickly can sometimes prevent deportation.

If a person with a detainer tried to pay their bond after the detainer has been issued, the jail will then turn them over to the government agency that issued the detainer.

If an alien has an ICE detainer and they make bond, they may be deported prior to their trial. This is why most judges will not issue a bond for illegal immigrants or people with ICE detainers.

If a person pays their bond but remains in jail waiting on a detainer, the jurisdiction that gave them the bond will NOT give the inmate time-served for the days they spend in jail after making bond. Once a person with a detainer makes bond, they are considered to be in the custody of the agency that issued the detainer.

If an inmate has to be in court in a different jurisdiction, that inmate must submit a transportation order or they may miss their court date. For example, if you are being held in Prince William County jail and are scheduled to appear in Arlington County court, your attorney should file a transportation order with the Arlington County court clerk's office several weeks before your court date.

Missing a court date because you did not file a transportation order can result in serious problems and additional criminal charges.

If you have multiple court dates in multiple jurisdictions, contact an attorney immediately. Transportation orders can take a long time to process.

Time Served
If you are put in jail prior to your court date, you will normally get time served for the time you spent in jail.

If you are held in a jail other than the county where you are facing charges, you will not get time served for those days until the jurisdiction where you are wanted submits a transportation order.

For example, if you have a warrant for your arrest in Fairfax County and you get picked up in Alexandria, then Fairfax County will not give you any credit for the time you spent in the Alexandria jail until Fairfax sends Alexandria a transportation order.

There can be major strategic benefits to controlling where you are held, when you file a transportation order, and when you pay a bond.

For example, a defendant is wanted in Fairfax for PWID marijuana but is arrested and held in Alexandria for DUI 2nd. The defendant talks to his attorney about both cases and they decide that he will likely get 10 days in jail for the DUI and 6 months in jail or more for the PWID in Fairfax. Under that scenario, the defendant may want to wait 10 days before submitting the transportation order, so that by the time of his trials he has served all his time in both jurisdictions.

It is also important to remember that each crime you are charged with comes with its own bond and its own time served.

For example, a defendant is arrested for DUI, possession of marijuana and possession of cocaine. The magistrate releases the defendant on recognizance on the marijuana charge, requires a $500 bond on the DUI charge and a $10,000 secured bond on the possession of cocaine. The defendant's girlfriend misunderstands and only pays the $500 bond after the defendant spends two days in jail. After a week, the defendant pays the remaining $10,000 bond and is then released from jail.

In this scenario, the defendant has served zero days for the marijuana charge, two days that can be applied to the DUI or possession of cocaine charge, and eight days that can only be applied to the possession of cocaine charge.

If the defendant in this scenario beats the DUI and the possession of cocaine charge and gets five days for the marijuana charge, then the defendant will not be able to use any of his time served.

Not all sheriff's departments calculate time served the same way. Talk to a local attorney to find out how your jurisdiction does it.

Calculating time served can be complicated. It is not uncommon for the sheriff's department or the court clerks to incorrectly calculate your release date. Make sure you hire an attorney who will help you if this happens to you. Fixing a release date error is very difficult without your attorney's help.

Chapter 12:
A Guide to Hiring an Attorney and Understanding Attorney-Client Contracts

It is important to hire an attorney *immediately* if you are charged with a crime. Most people do not realize that some of their defenses expire long before trial. If you do not have an attorney to file specific paperwork before the expiration date, you lose the chance to make those defenses.

Never put off hiring an attorney. Additionally, a criminal defense attorney can help you get out on bond or lower your bond – but only if you hire them soon enough.

Besides, you usually pay the same amount for an attorney no matter when you hire them. Why not get more service for your money and hire the attorney sooner?

Getting a Continuance to Hire an Attorney
If your trial date is approaching and you still do not have an attorney, most courts will allow you one or two continuances in order to find representation. However, using continuances for this purpose can be dangerous. In addition to losing the opportunity to make certain defenses, you may also lose the right to receive future continuances. You are allowed a limited number of continuances. If you use all of your continuances finding an attorney, then you will not have any left for the trial.

Continuances are very important and should never be wasted. Continuances can be used to discover what evidence the prosecution has against you. In many jurisdictions, your attorney cannot talk to the police or commonwealth attorney to discover their evidence against you until the actual day of the trial. When your attorney cannot see the evidence against you until the day of the trial, then continuances are needed in order to prepare a defense.

Also, receiving a continuance may increase the odds that the court will grant the prosecuting attorneys a continuance if they ask for it. If the police officer or a laboratory technician does not show up at the trial, the prosecution will likely ask for a continuance in order to prevent the case from being dismissed. If the court has already granted you several continuances, the court may be more likely grant the prosecution a continuance as well.

Do not put yourself in a position where you or your attorney will have to waste continuances. Find an attorney immediately.

Typical Fee Structures
Most (but not all) criminal defense attorneys in Virginia charge a flat fee and demand that the fee be paid before they agree to represent you.

These fees usually do not cover any court expenses (such as hiring a court reporter, gathering evidence, serving process, or hiring expert witnesses). Court reporters and process servers can cost hundreds of dollars while expert witnesses can cost thousands of extra dollars. Discuss the possibility of needing these services before you sign an attorney-client contract.

Some attorneys also have different rates for appeals, certain motions, continuances, going to trial versus taking a plea, jury trial versus a trial without a jury. It is very important to read the fine print of your attorney-client contract and discuss the possibility of being charged for these extra expenses.

Post-Trial Services
Some attorney-client contracts end as soon as the judge makes a ruling. When those clients walk out of the courtroom, they no longer have an attorney. In this situation the attorney may not be obligated to aid the client in registering for probation, getting their bail back, paying fines, or appealing their conviction.

If you are convicted of a crime there is a significant chance that you could be sentenced to additional jail time if you fail to comply with the terms of your probation, the terms of your restricted license, or other conditions imposed by the judge. An attorney can be invaluable in helping you navigate the post-conviction process. Always make sure your retention agreement defines post-conviction responsibilities.

Beginning and Ending an Attorney-Client Relationship
It is extremely important for the attorney and the client to clearly define how and when their relationship will begin and end. It is also important to define what conditions will terminate an agreement. Can your attorney drop you as a client? Can you switch attorneys if you are not satisfied? If you terminate the agreement will your money be refunded? What happens if your attorney becomes sick or otherwise unavailable? These questions should be clearly addressed in the retention agreement.

Orders of Substitution
If you ever want to change attorneys, your new attorney must file an order of substitution with the court. However, the motion for an order of substitution requires the signature of the old attorney, the new attorney, the defendant, the judge, and in some cases the signature of the prosecution as well. This process can take quite a bit of time so if you are not satisfied with your attorney, do not wait to find a new one.

Chapter 13:
How to Spot a Bad Attorney and What to Look for in a Good One

Picking the right attorney for you and your case is a very personal decision. While there is no formula to finding the perfect attorney, this chapter contains a list of things to consider while looking for an attorney.

Get a Free Consultation and Use It Effectively
Almost every criminal defense attorney offers a free consultation (by phone or in person). Use the consultation to get to know your attorney. Before meeting with an attorney make a list of questions you have for them and write down the important details of your case.

Read the Contract Carefully
The attorney you hire is only as good as the contract you sign. The retention agreement will spell out what the attorney will and will not do for you.

Make sure the attorney you hire will walk you through at least some of the post-conviction processes and appeal your case if needed. Some defendants who attempt to navigate the post-trial process without an attorney end up getting arrested because they don't understand what the law required them to do. Remember, it does not matter how good an attorney is if the contract does not require them to help you.

What Does Your Attorney Specialize in?
There are many different types of law that a lawyer can practice but only so many hours in the day that an attorney

can spend studying the forensic and legal issues of criminal defense. Have a frank and open discussion about how many criminal defense cases your attorney does on a regular basis. Talk to your attorney about what they do to increase and update their knowledge of criminal law and forensic issues.

Because criminal law is so complicated and because the laws changes so frequently, it can be essential to hire an attorney who invests substantial time and resources learning about the forensic and constitutional issues that are unique to drug crimes.

Who Will Be Working on Your Case?
Sometimes the attorney who interviews you is not the attorney who represents you at the trial. Have a frank discussion about how your case will be delegated and who will be representing you at court.

Having multiple attorneys working on your case can be a good thing. However, make sure you understand what each attorney's role will be and, if possible, interview all attorneys who will be working on your case before signing a contract.

Does Your Attorney Have Enough Time?
Most of the mistakes made by attorneys happen because those attorneys are too busy, not because they are inexperienced or incompetent. Your attorney needs to have all the facts of the case and understand how the various consequences of conviction will affect you. There is no substitute for spending time talking with your attorney. If

you do not feel like you have had enough time to talk, get another attorney.

Do I Trust My Attorney?
Because most of an attorney's job happens outside the courtroom, most of what an attorney does is done behind closed doors. You cannot watch your attorney 24/7 and you should never feel you must micromanage your attorney. If you do not feel comfortable trusting your attorney with your case, you should get another attorney.

Does Your Attorney Empower You?
An attorney is a counselor, not a ruler. The attorney's job is to explain options and consequences to the client and thus empower the client to make informed decisions. Empowering a client to make informed decisions is a process that begins at the very first meeting.

Make sure you hire an attorney who you feel is good at listening, asking questions, and explaining. Once again, there is no substitute for spending time talking to your attorney.

Does Your Attorney Care?
The second biggest complaint I hear from defendants is that their attorney does not care. Criminal defense can be a very emotionally demanding profession. It can be difficult to constantly empathize with clients' circumstances.

If you feel your attorney is not concerned about your problems, hire another attorney.

What is Their Experience?

When it comes to experience, it is quality, not quantity that matters. It is not a bad idea to find out how much experience they have with your type of case. How much experience do they have in your jurisdiction? How will their particular experiences affect their ability to represent you? It may also be informative to talk to your attorney about what aspects of your case would be new for them.

Is Your Lawyer Detail Oriented?

When it comes to criminal defense, the devil is in the details. I saw this firsthand as a new attorney when I watched a defendant go to jail for five days simply because his defense attorney did not notice a typo on the plea agreement. As the bailiff dragged the confused and terrified man to jail, the judge told the attorney that they should have read the agreement more carefully. *You do not want this to happen to you!*

Use the free consultation period to gauge how detail-oriented your attorney is. I am also a firm believer that how attorneys take care of themselves and their offices says a lot about how detail-oriented they are in their profession as well.

Hire the Best Attorney You Can Afford

Try to keep price comparisons in perspective when shopping for an attorney. Do not make the mistake of hiring your second choice just to save a few dollars.

Also, always compare fee structures as well as services. Will your attorney handle an appeal for free or will they charge you? Is there a different fee for trials versus pleas? Is there a fee for jury trial? Is there a fee if the case goes beyond a preliminary hearing? It is usually a good idea to budget for the possibility of a trial and an appeal.

If the attorney who is the best fit for you is out of your price range do not give up. Have an open and honest discussion with that attorney about your financial situation. Some attorneys may choose to offer payment plans or pro bono services.

People Skills Are Important

Before you go to trial, your attorney will have a chance to talk the prosecution into giving you what you want. At the trial, your attorney will try to get the judge to give you what you want. Trials and plea negotiations are all about people skills.

The best attorneys are friendly, confident, and assertive. They can demand respect while treating others respectfully. If an attorney bad-mouths judges, prosecutors, or other attorneys, odds are that those same people are bad-mouthing him.

Is My Attorney Honest and Ethical?

The courts in Virginia have long memories, and a lawyer who is not trusted may be a detriment to your case. You will be placing a large amount of trust in the person you hire to represent you.

Look for those attorneys who have the highest ethical and moral standards. If you have doubts about the integrity of your counselor, consider looking elsewhere.

Chapter 14
Preparing For Your Trial

Whether you are planning on fighting your case to the end, or taking a deal, here are some things you should always discuss with your attorney in order to prepare for your trial.

Write Down Your Version of Events
I always recommend to my clients that they write down everything they can remember regarding their case as soon as possible. It is important to preserve your memories before they fade, and to send them in writing to your attorney. Any time you do this, clearly write: "Confidential Attorney-Client Communication" across the top.

Writing down your story not only preserves your memory, but also enhances communication with your attorney. Forgotten facts, miscommunications, and simple mistakes are less likely if you write everything down and send it to your attorney as soon as possible.

Write Down a Bio About Yourself
Your attorney needs to know you just as much as he needs to know your case. Write down a little about yourself. Criminal history (juvenile and adult), job, family, and hobbies are all very important.

Having an accurate criminal history is extremely important, but knowing interesting facts about a client can also be very useful in humanizing that client in the eyes of judges, jurors, and prosecutors. Let your attorney know who you are and put it in writing.

Rehab/Drug Treatment

If you have been arrested for drug possession, you need to quit using all drugs immediately. Pre-trial release, your pre-sentencing interview, and your probation may require you to undergo drug testing. Picking up another drug charge would also be a major blow to your case, your bail, and could result in severe consequences.

You need to be clean and sober while you are waiting for your trial. If you are not able to avoid drug use for the entire time, do not be afraid to seek help. Drug treatment can help you gain control over your life as well as help your case during sentencing.

For simple possession cases, completing community service, drug treatment, and undergoing private drug testing to prove sobriety can be used to convince a prosecutor to drop or severely reduce your charges.

If you decide to seek drug or alcohol treatment keep a journal of what treatment you are receiving, when you received it, where you received it, and what you got out of it.

Do not be afraid to include your thoughts and feelings regarding your substance abuse issues. These journals can become powerful tools that your attorney can use to help the judge appreciate what you are going through and what you have accomplished.

For a list of rehab options, read the chapter on drug rehabilitation.

Rehearse with Your Attorney

Whether you want to be a witness at your own trial, or whether you want to address the judge during the sentencing day, it is important to practice what you are going to say. Write down what you want to say, discuss it with your attorney, and practice.

Defendants who seriously attend Alcoholics Anonymous or Narcotics Anonymous often do very well at this. AA and NA help because AA and NA meetings center on members talking to groups about their addictions and rehabilitation goals. Regular participants tend to be more articulate and honest about their issues and this can often impress even the more skeptical judges.

Prepare a Restricted License Application Before Sentencing

Defendants should always prepare a restricted license application with their attorney before the trial. This is an important and complex application that should not be done hastily.

Most drug charges come with a six-month loss of driving privileges. In some situations you may be able to get a restricted license to drive to and from work, school, church, doctors, probation visits, and a few other activities.

To apply for a restricted license, the driver will need to provide the court with the exact times and locations of the places to which they need to drive (such as work and church). If the driver wants to drive to work, health care providers, school, or day care, they must provide documentation containing the specific times and locations.

The judge may or may not grant the restricted license, or the judge may grant it under conditions of the court's choosing. This can be problematic for clients who go to work at different times or locations each day. The more complicated your work schedule, the less likely it is that a judge will give you a restricted license. It is essential to have an attorney available to help with the application process.

If a driver is not happy with their restricted license or if they need to change their restricted license, they may make a motion to amend their license.

Make sure you know whether your attorney-client contract guarantees your attorney's help in getting and/or amending a restricted license.

Once a driver gets a restricted license, he must carry it with him whenever he drives. Furthermore, he may only drive during the times stated on the license and between the locations approved on the license.

The restricted license issued by the court is printed on a green 8.5" x 11" piece of paper. This license is a temporary restricted license. The driver has 60 days to go to the DMV and get a permanent (plastic) restricted license before the court's temporary restricted license expires.

If a defendant has a commercial driver's license (CDL), the DMV will not issue a restricted license even if the judge approves it. If you have a CDL, make sure that you inform your attorney as soon as possible.

Chapter 15:
Pros and Cons of Appealing a Conviction

When a person is arrested for a misdemeanor in Virginia, he is tried in the General District Court (GDC) of the county, city, or town where the crime was committed. A conviction in GDC can be appealed to the Circuit Court of Virginia within ten calendar days.

An appeal to the Circuit Court is an appeal by right, meaning that the defendant only has to ask for an appeal to get one. No one can deny the defendant an appeal as long as it is filed properly within ten days.

If the defendant appeals to the Circuit Court, several things will happen. The GDC judge may issue an appeal bond if the defendant was sentenced to jail, and the GDC's sentence and conviction will be erased. This means that the driver's license will be returned and the driver will be released from custody once an appeal bond is paid.

Be sure to make arrangements for your attorney to help you with your appeal prior to your trial in General District Court. If you have already retained your attorney for your appeal and you are sentenced to jail in the lower court, your attorney can usually prevent you from having to go to jail.

If you have not made such arrangements, then you may have to arrange to retain your attorney or file your own appeal while sitting in jail. This may result in spending unnecessary time behind bars.

Your new trial will be held in the Circuit Court. The Circuit Court will conduct a completely new trial. The Circuit Court judges are not bound by any decision made by the GDC judge. A Circuit Court judge can punish a driver more leniently, more severely, or not at all. This is called a trial *de novo*.

The Circuit Court is a different court system than the General District Court. The Circuit Court has different procedural rules. For example, you can get a jury trial in Circuit Court, but you cannot have one in GDC.

The Circuit Court in some jurisdictions is located in a different building or even a different city than GDC, so make sure you know where you are supposed to go on the day of your appeal.

There are additional court costs associated with Circuit Court. Circuit Court can also have different requirements for getting a restricted driver's license so talk to your attorney before appealing.

The decisions of the Circuit Court can be appealed to the Virginia Court of Appeals and then to the Supreme Court of Virginia. However, these courts can choose whether or not to hear those appeals. The Court of Appeals and Virginia Supreme Court will only reverse decisions by the Circuit Court if the Circuit Court made a serious mistake.

Motions to Reconsider
If you are convicted and sentenced you may be able to ask the judge to reconsider the punishment.

A motion to reconsider can only be granted if the court still has jurisdiction over the defendant. In General District Court, a judge loses jurisdiction to reconsider if the case is appealed to Circuit Court or if, after 60 days, it is not appealed.

A Circuit Court judge loses jurisdiction to reconsider a case if the defendant is transported to the Department of Corrections (i.e. prison).

Prior to filing a motion to reconsider in Circuit Court, an attorney can file a motion to stay transportation, which can prevent the court from losing jurisdiction.

Motions to reconsider should be based on new information that was not previous available at the first sentencing hearing. Post-sentencing mental health diagnosis, completion of drug treatment programs or rehab may be examples of new information that may influence a judge to reconsider.

If you believe you should file a motion to reconsider, consult an attorney immediately before your opportunity expires.

Chapter 16
Drug Treatment and Rehabilitation

If you have been arrested for drug possession, you need to quit using drugs and alcohol immediately. Your pre-trial release, pre-sentencing interview, and probation may require you to undergo drug and/or alcohol testing. Failing one of those drug tests can have serious consequences.

If you are not able to completely avoid using drugs while awaiting your trial, don't be afraid to seek help. Drug treatment can help you gain control over your life as well as help your criminal case.

Prolonged sobriety is a big achievement and many judges take notice when a defendant proactively seeks help with addiction. If drug treatment is going to be part of your probation or bond, proactively seeking help before being ordered to do so can give you the freedom to choose the type of treatment you receive and benefits you during sentencing.

Drug treatment and rehabilitation can take many forms and deal with many different issues. Drug treatment can be particularly helpful if you are also dealing with alcohol abuse, mental health issues, or emotional burdens.

The first step is to talk to your primary health care provider for local recommendations. Your insurance provider may also provide coverage and recommendations for substance abuse treatment. Some local sources for substance abuse treatment are also listed below.

Alcoholics Anonymous (AA) & Narcotic Anonymous (NA)
If you are not sure whether treatment is necessary, Alcoholics Anonymous (AA) or Narcotics Anonymous (NA) may be an excellent place to start. AA and NA meetings can be found in cities all over the country.

AA and NA meetings are free and strictly confidential. You can show up to a meeting and just listen without commitment or obligation. You can find a local AA or NA meeting online at www.aa.org or www.na.org

I am a big advocate of AA and NA. People who get involved in AA and NA group meetings and really embrace the program consistently receive less severe punishments. AA and NA meetings teach a person how to articulate their addiction issues and their goals for recovery. Listing to an AA or NA participant talk honestly about their substance abuse issues can be very moving even for a judge.

Virginia Community Service Board
In Virginia, each local government has a local community service board that is in charge of coordinating mental health and substance abuse treatment services in that locality. Most localities offer extremely discounted or free treatment. These programs are an excellent starting point for someone (rich or poor) who is looking for mental health or substance abuse treatment. Each locality's program is different but most only treat residents of that locality. Waiting periods can be long so do not procrastinate signing up for a treatment evaluation.

A list of some of the local programs is included in this chapter. For a complete list of all of the community service boards in Virginia, go to: www.dbhds.virginia.gov

Maryland Department of Health and Hygiene
The Maryland Department of Health and Hygiene's Alcohol and Drug Abuse Administration has county drug and alcohol treatment programs and lists private facilities with state certifications on their website. Each county has their own Department of Health and Hygiene substance abuse programs. For lists of these programs and lists of certified treatment facilities, go to: http://adaa.dhmh.maryland.gov

Nar-Anon Family Groups
Nar-Anon is not for addicts. Nar-Anon is for the relatives and friends of addicts. Nar-Anon is a twelve-step program designed to help relatives and friends of addicts recover from the effects of coping with an addicted relative or friend. Nar-Anon's program of recovery uses Nar-Anon's Twelve Steps and Twelve Traditions. The only requirement to be a member and attend Nar-Anon meetings is that there is a problem of drugs or addiction in a relative or friend. Nar-Anon is not affiliated with any other organization or outside entity. There is no cost or dues associated with attending a Nar-Anon meeting. More information and local Nar-Anon meetings can be found online at www.nar-anon.org.

Northern Virginia, Maryland, and DC Substance Abuse Treatment Centers

Arlington County Community Services Board
Behavioral Healthcare

1725 N. George Mason Drive
Arlington, VA 22205
703-228-4900

This program services residents of Arlington, Arlington's homeless, people receiving Medicaid, or inmates in the Arlington County Adult Detention Center. Programs include residential treatment and case management support for adults with substance abuse problems. Individuals are evaluated by case management staff and placed in the appropriate level of residential treatment. Sliding fees are based on income.

Alexandria Community Services Board
Substance Abuse Services

2355 Mill Road Suite A
Alexandria, VA 22314
703-746-3600

This is detox center with a 30-day outpatient program. There are also programs that service individuals with HIV/AIDS, inmates, and individuals suffering from a combination of substance abuse and mental health issues.

Fairfax County Detoxification Center

4213 Walney Road Chantilly, VA 20151
703-502-7000

The Fairfax County Detoxification center serves only
Fairfax County and Falls Church residents. They provide
inpatient, outpatient and even over-the-phone counseling for
substance abuse issues. The Fairfax County Detoxification
Center is one of the best community service board programs
in northern Virginia and is an excellent place to begin
seeking help if you live in Fairfax or Falls Church. All
services cost only $30.

Prince William County Community Services Board

703-792-7800 in Manassas
703-792-4900 in Woodbridge

The Prince William County CSB offers substance abuse and
mental health treatment for county residents. They offer
group therapy, individual treatment, inpatient, and outpatient
resources. They also have special programs for inmates,
youth, and women (particularly pregnant women). Fees are
based on ability to pay.

Loudoun County Mental Health Center
Substance Abuse Program

102 Heritage Way NE Mailstop # 77A

Leesburg, VA 20175
703-771-5100
703-777-0320 (emergency number)

Services adolescents, people with co-occurring mental and substance abuse disorders, women, men, and inmates.

Rappahannock-Rapidan Community Services Board

Culpeper County: 540-825-5656
Fauquier County: 540-347-7620
Madison County: 540-948-5911
Orange County: 540-672-2718
Rappahannock County: 540-675-3329

Includes motivational enhancement therapy, individual psychotherapy, education groups, group therapy, women's alternatives (an intensive outpatient program for chemically dependent women), drug screening, acupuncture, and case management services. On recommendation from the local community service board, patients may be referred to the Boxwood Recovery Center. The Boxwood Recovery Center is a 28-day residential alcohol and other drug treatment program. The referring community service board may request a variable length of stay from two weeks to 60 days.

Rappahannock Community Services Board

Caroline County Clinic
19254 Rogers Clark Blvd.

Ruther Glen, VA 22546
804-633-9997

Fredericksburg Clinic
600 Jackson Street
Fredericksburg, VA 22401
540-373-3223

King George County Clinic
8479 St Anthonys Road
King George, VA 22485
540-775-9879

Spotsylvania County Clinic
7424 Brock Road
Spotsylvania, VA 22553
540-582-3980

Stafford County Clinic
15 Hope Road
Stafford, VA 22554
540-659-2725

Contact the local community service board for details regarding services.

---

*Partners in Drug Abuse Rehabilitation
and Counseling (PIDARC) (Washington DC)*

2112 F Street NW Suite 102

Washington, DC 20037
202-296-4455 x3202

This is an outpatient treatment facility with programs for people with co-occurring mental and substance abuse disorders, pregnant/postpartum women, and anyone else.

Mental Health Substance Abuse Program
La Clinica del Pueblo Inc (Washington DC)

2831 15th Street NW
Washington, DC 20009
http://www.lcdp.org
202-462-4788 x241

This is an outpatient treatment facility with programs for persons with co-occurring mental and substance abuse disorders, inmates, and Spanish speaking patients.

Phoenix House (Arlington, Va.)

200 North Glebe Road,
Arlington, VA 22203
703-841-0703
1-800-DRUG-HELP

This is a private treatment facility with multiple locations in Arlington, VA. Phoenix House offers specialized programs for pregnant women, teens, Spanish speakers, men and women. These facilities provide residential treatment that can allow people to work or go to school during the day and return for testing, treatment, and counseling sessions. Phoenix House has other location across the east coast.

A Woman's Place (Fredericksburg)

2016 Lafayette Boulevard, Suite 101
Fredericksburg, VA 22401
540-891-3136

This is an intensive program with outpatient, psycho-education, and weekly treatment groups. This program has specialized individual and group therapy services for women; linkage to community resources; placements to residential treatment and coordination of services, especially with criminal justice and social service agencies.

MRB Counseling Services (Maryland)

Frederick Office
5 Hillcrest Dr, Suite B200
Frederick, MD 21703
Ph: 240-566-5656 / 301-378-2929
Fax: 301-378-2930

Gaithersburg Office
317 E Diamond Ave, Suite C
Gaithersburg, MD 20877
Ph: 301-527-0854 / 301-512-0663
Fax: 240-243-1061